HOT MESS
KITCHEN

HOT MESS
KITCHEN

Recipes for Your
Delicious
Disastrous Life

Gabi Moskowitz and Miranda Berman
PHOTOGRAPHS BY FRANKIE FRANKENY

GRAND CENTRAL
Life & Style
NEW YORK • BOSTON

Grand Central Life & Style
Hachette Book Group
1290 Avenue of the Americas, New York, NY 10104
grandcentrallifeandstyle.com
twitter.com/grandcentralpub

First Edition: September 2017

Grand Central Life & Style is an imprint of Grand Central Publishing. The Grand Central Life & Style name and logo are trademarks of Hachette Book Group, Inc.

The publisher is not responsible for websites (or their content) that are not owned by the publisher.

The Hachette Speakers Bureau provides a wide range of authors for speaking events. To find out more, go to www.hachettespeakersbureau.com or call (866) 376-6591.

Brand names and trademarks used in this book are the property of their respective owners. Use of them is not intended to imply any affiliation with or endorsement of the book by the owners.

Print book interior design by Elizabeth Van Itallie.

Library of Congress Cataloging-in-Publication Data
Names: Moskowitz, Gabi, author. | Berman, Miranda, editor.
Title: Hot mess kitchen : recipes for your delicious disastrous life / Gabi Moskowitz and Miranda Berman ; photographs by Frankie Frankeny.
Description: New York : Grand Central Life & Style, [2017] | Includes index.
Identifiers: LCCN 2016057331| ISBN 9781455596508 (hardcover) | ISBN 9781455596515 (ebook)
Subjects: LCSH: Cooking. | LCGFT: Cookbooks.
Classification: LCC TX714 .M6797 2017 | DDC 641.5—dc23 LC record available at https://lccn.loc.gov/2016057331

ISBNs: 978-1-4555-9650-8 (hardcover), 978-1-4555-9651-5 (ebook)

Printed in the United States of America

Q-MA

10 9 8 7 6 5 4 3 2 1

FOR MY HUSBAND, EVAN,
WHOSE LOVE MAKES EVERY DAY BRIGHTER,
SWEETER, AND MORE DELICIOUS.
—GLM

FOR MY PARENTS, RUSSELL AND ANITA,
WHOM I LOVE VERY MUCH.
THEY HAVE SEEN ME THROUGH MY MESSIEST
MOMENTS AND THEY ARE NOT ALLOWED
TO READ THIS BOOK.
—MPB

CONTENTS

FOREWORD

by Mindy Kaling

I wish I was a hot mess. Looking back on my twenties* you probably could've described me as an "anxious mess," a "workaholic mess," or maybe just a plain "mess mess." Unfortunately, I lacked the sexy confidence it would have taken to qualify me as a hot one. So when Miranda and Gabi gave me their book, I was so excited. Reading it felt so aspirational. If I can't be a hot mess, at least I want to learn all the secrets of two bona fide ones (who also happen to be adorable and chic and blond).

And who wouldn't be excited to tear into *Hot Mess Kitchen*? This book is awesome. I came for the recipes and stayed for the funny, personal writing. How could you not love a book with recipes like "Fuck It, Let's Just Get Stoned Nachos" and "All My Friends Are Married Mud Pie"? Surely there is not one among you who has not felt both sentiments. You could buy this book and enjoy it without ever taking out your oven mitts.

But not me! I take my foreword-writing seriously, and I wanted to test out some recipes. A word about me: When it comes to cooking, I am really basic. I like things really obvious and hard to mess up. The extent of my cooking in my twenties was a piece of steak flattened into submission on my George Foreman Grill, then covered in Tabasco sauce. So I was a little worried about testing these out. The great news? They're legit and they're easy AF (am I using that acronym right? I'm old). My personal favorites were "Schadenfreude Sundae" and the "Netflix and Chili Con Carne." If you think it sounds a little sad that I made a batch of delicious chili and ate it while watching *Narcos* alone on my sofa, then you don't know just how good that recipe is. I feel sad for *you*.

This is a great gift for your young, coolest friends and an even better gift for yourself. I can't wait for you to get your copy and promptly cover it in food stains, as I did. Joyfully.

---

*I'm still, like, twenty-seven.

WELCOME TO OUR BOOK

Hello, beautiful reader,

Gabi and Miranda here. Welcome to our book! Thanks for buying it! Or maybe your cool aunt bought it for you as a graduation gift? Perhaps the delivery guy who drops off your weekly burrito gave it to you passive-aggressively with your last order? Maybe your mom sent it to you after having hacked into your email account and deciding you were incompetent. Are you yelling at your mom right now? Stop! Forgive her. But just for buying you this book (because you will like it). No need to forgive her for anything else. You can blame your parents, or anyone else, forever and never assume responsibility for anything! It will be healthy and fun. Just kidding. Unfortunately, at some point, you do have to grow up and take care of yourself. We know, we know, this is truly a horrific endeavor (no matter how old you actually are), so we're here to help by teaching you how to cook. We're not asking you to open your mail every day or even to go through the giant stack of papers sitting on your bedroom floor. We're merely suggesting that you think about learning how to cook.

Keep reading! Don't run away because cooking seems scary and/or you're lazy. We get it and we agree: doing basically anything is terrifying. What are plans? Do you stick with them? You do? You've *left* the house before? Whoa. Well, for the rest of us slackers, we're going to demonstrate how to cook fun, tasty, mostly healthy food in a manageable way so that you actually do it when you say you will. The trick is breaking things down into steps and doing a little bit at a time, starting with what to buy at the grocery store and going all the way to using your culinary skills to trick someone into falling in love with you forever.

Cooking is a thing you can do to truly treat yourself well. Do you have some vision of a perfect, put-together, chic, awesome version of yourself? Are you worried you'll never become her? The only way you will is if you start acting like her now. You, lovely reader, deserve to have a nice meal when you come home from work, or wherever you go during the day (we don't judge). It will make you feel better. We promise. Okay, we know this is all very corny, and we're sorry about that. We promise the rest of the book won't be like this. Okay, it might have some moments, but everyone just chill.

And we're going to be here every step of the way, telling you which knife to use and how to tell if your meat is ready or if you'll be getting salmonella (relax, you *probably* won't). We'll be there when your mascara is running because you're chopping onions, or because you're crying, or because you sneezed right after applying it. And we're going to sprinkle all our recipes with interesting musings and embarrassing anecdotes to keep you entertained. We're going to be your friends. Your kitchen friends, your hot mess kitchen friends. Your best friends? No, no, this isn't like a *Her* type of scenario. Have real friends.

We're excited to hang.
XOXO,
Gabi and Miranda

FUTURE LOVERS!

MPB

Before we get deep into the cooking, Gabi and I want to introduce ourselves properly. You've got to be wondering who the hell we are and why you should bother listening to us. Well, I'm a comedy writer living in Los Angeles and Gabi is an accomplished chef. Gabi will be our sage cook throughout this book and I will be our more novice hot mess chef.

So, I'll start with my hot-messness. One of my main problems in life is that I really do not want to grow up. In my adolescence, I'd wake up crying in the middle of the night realizing I was going to age and eventually have to leave my parents' home. I'd like to be a true baby forever. My calculations have proven this impossible, so I've begrudgingly aged, fighting it harshly every step of the way. Refusal to accept certain responsibilities has left me acting like a hot mess for most of my twenties.

Sure, there are times when being a hot mess is fun and glamorous, like in a mainstream romantic comedy, but then there are also times when it's really fucking terrible, like in an indie romantic comedy. I once ate dirt after seeing a YouTube video of someone else doing it. And it wasn't even the right kind of dirt. It's supposed to be, like, clay and I ate from a potted plant. I've never gone into full self-destruct mode in a visible way, although doing so seems very old-Hollywood chic, but I've never really taken care of myself in a serious way either, until recently.

I'd already been going to therapy and had even downloaded a meditation app on my phone (and used it like three times), but I still needed to make changes to my everyday life. I needed to do things like sleep in feet-softening gel socks every night, actually finish *Infinite Jest*, and finally, I needed to learn how to cook. (Probably never going to finish *IJ*.)

My mother rarely cooked when I was growing up, and when she did, she'd yell at me to get out of the kitchen. I also am pretty certain I was born without motor skills. I do love mixing things together though. Like, I was always the friend who put too much extra shit in the cake batter so no one would eat it. My friends thought I was sloppy and disgusting. I thought I was creative and that I might grow up to be a fairly decent chef. I was right. And if I can cook, then you can cook.

And I swear you will like it, or I hope you will like it. Honestly, sometimes just opening my pantry to see that I have flour in my house reminds me that I'm a human. Noticing dirty dishes in my sink reminds me that I had friends over for dinner last night and that I *probably* won't die alone. Cooking also can distract you from your problems when you're in a panic. It makes people like you and makes you want to entertain. Most importantly, it's a great way to seduce people.

Are you still not convinced that you can cook? Okay, well then: read this book, and all our stories, and let us show you how cooking has helped us, or how it could have helped us, in our messiest moments.

I love you and the person who bought you this book, but I promise to always love you more.

I THINK WE'RE GOING TO LIKE EACH OTHER

GLM

Miranda and I wrote this book because, in separate ways, we each discovered that cooking is an excellent way to take control when life feels out of control. For her, it was a lesson that came in her midtwenties. For me, it started when I was a little girl.

I was a sensitive, moody, and probably clinically depressed kid. I was smart and creative, but I had a hard time fitting in. When I was eight, my mother bought me an antique set of pots and pans to play with. I begged to use them for *real* cooking, so she gave me her copy of Mollie Katzen's *The Enchanted Broccoli Forest* and let me try my hand at some simple dishes.

In the kitchen, with my little mixing bowls, frying pan, and kid-size chef's knife, I learned to dice, chop, bake, and sauté. I learned to trust my instincts with flavor combinations, putting my own stamp on recipes. I learned that if I could taste, I could cook—it was just a matter of learning a few simple techniques and being a little bit brave. The world was hard and scary, but the kitchen was a safe place where I could always be myself, and where my hard work was rewarded with something delicious.

Growing up has made some things easier (I made cool, like-minded friends and finally got those boobs I had been wishing for) and, of course, some things a lot harder. When I was in my early twenties, I floated from dead-end job to dead-end job, regularly overdrew my checking account, and slept with men who didn't respect me. I was testing the boundaries, feeling my way through life, trying to get my bearings, and often failing. But through it all, at the end of every shitty, exhilarating, hilarious, disastrous day, I cooked dinner in my tiny apartment kitchen. And, just as it had when I was a little girl, it made me feel better.

Today, like just about every other woman I know, I spend my days oscillating between thinking I am amazing and questioning my worth. I am sometimes impulsive and sometimes so anxious about everything that I become immobile. We live in a world where advertisers, TV, magazines, and insane Instagram filters blast us with nonstop messages about what is wrong with us. We are told to be thin, but not *too* thin! Fun, but not irresponsible! Strong, but not so much that it's threatening! Feminine *and* feminist, but not too much so! Have it all! But don't take too much! It's enough to make anyone feel crazy.

I hope this book helps make the craziness that lives both inside and outside of you more manageable. I can't promise it will ever go away, but I do know that taming it is possible—and delicious.

HOT MESS
KITCHEN

GETTING STARTED
WELCOME TO YOUR KITCHEN!
IT'S OKAY IF YOU'VE NEVER
BEEN IN HERE BEFORE. GLM

Have a seat at your kitchen table, pour yourself a cup of coffee, tea, or vodka—whatever soothes you—and get ready to get cooking. Look around. Welcome to your kitchen! In case you two are still in the initial phases of getting to know each other, allow me to show you around.

This big boxy thing is your stove. You'll boil, sauté, and fry up top, and down below you'll find your oven. This is where your cookies will crisp up, your chickens will roast, and your mac and cheese will bubble and brown. Show it love by keeping it clean. It will love you back.

Real quick: Go find your broiler. Is it above the top rack of your oven? Or is it the old-fashioned kind, a pullout beneath the oven door? If it's the latter, do not attempt to store baking sheets there—they will warp and then your cookies will slide right off them. Or plastic containers: If you're like Miranda, who foolishly stored Tupperware down there, forgot about it, tried to make lasagna, and then was treated to the stench of burning plastic, you will completely fuck up your cookware, break your oven, and have to make an awkward call to your landlord. Learn from Miranda's mistakes.

Found it? Good. The broiler is the G-spot of the kitchen: hard to find, but once you do, things get a whole lot more fun!

Okay, moving on. Let's check out your fridge. This frosty rectangle should be where your fresh foods are kept fresh longer. Is it crusted with leftover lo mein and aging yogurt? Is there an indecipherable smell coming from your veggie bin? Better give it some loving.

Take everything out. Toss anything you're unsure about or that is clearly not good anymore. (Do not feel guilty about throwing away your roommate's moldy cottage cheese—if she cared so much about it she would have eaten before 11/3/13, when it expired.) Once everything that needs to go has gone, give it a thorough scrub-down.

Now give the same treatment to your pantry and any other cupboards you use to store food. Clear out the old stuff, wipe down the shelves, and make sure the only food left in there is usable. (We know you think you'll eventually finish all four of those half-eaten bags of stale tortilla chips—you won't.)

All good? Good. Now let's fill it with all the good stuff. First, the basics.

TIME TO MAKE YOUR LITTLE HOUSE A LITTLE HOME WITH A LITTLE KITCHEN THAT YOU USE

MPB

Hi there, you budding chefs de cuisine. Get ready for your first very moving personal tale, the purpose of which is to push you into buying pots and pans and stocking your pantry. I swear we don't have some deal with the pots and pans company, but maybe we should. (Note to editor: Talk to Mrs. Potts from *Beauty and the Beast*. I feel like she'll get our vibe and cut us a deal. Cartoon Mrs. Potts *or* Emma Thompson will work. I'm sure she has time for this.)

My only criterion for my first apartment in LA was "shortest lease possible." I had a job I was excited about, but I still wanted to be able to pick up from my life at a moment's notice and run far away, like to Dubai or something. Not only was I afraid of being alone, but I also had paralyzingly high expectations for what my life should look like. I wanted my first apartment to be perfect and it wouldn't be, so I figured why bother trying at all.

My lack of effort best manifested itself in the kitchen. I did not stock my fridge. I only had vodka. I romanticized it by thinking of myself as Holly Golightly in *Breakfast at Tiffany's*. Unfortunately, I'm allergic to cats and also I hate them, so I bought a stuffed animal cat and called it Cat and went about my business.

Once a week, I would go to a specialty store and buy a fancy piece of cheese, jam, and some premade tuna salad. This reminded me of my parents' house. Fancy cheese and pretty jam were my security blanket. I slept with them at night. Sure, my sheets were sticky, but whenever friends came over they thought I was having a lot of sex. They also thought I was disgusting.

If I didn't have real food, I certainly didn't have any pots, pans, or cookware. I mean, what would I have used them for? Like, a ska band? A place to store my drugs? Those were already in the oven. I was fine. Frankly, I didn't want to pay for anything I wouldn't need at the exact moment in time I was at the store buying it. I also didn't want to do any research. Was a cookie sheet really necessary? Was I a bad person if I didn't have a gorgeous cast iron skillet? What is a heavy-bottomed pan? Was I a heavy-bottomed pan? (I think so.) These easily Googleable questions were too daunting to deal with, so I ignored them like they were a guy who was super into me and wouldn't stop texting. I was living paycheck to paycheck, taking out, and basically squatting in an apartment where I paid rent. I truly was a hot mess, but it wasn't even remotely hot.

. . . Until six months went by and my landlord asked me if I wanted to sign a one-year lease. If I didn't, she'd have to find someone else who would, and I'd have to move and do the exact same thing all over again. I realized I had to admit I lived in Los Angeles, and I wasn't going home to Mom and Dad, or to Dubai (for the moment, anyway). I signed the lease. That night I stopped sleeping with cheese and jam. I also decided it was a good time to start stocking my fridge and cabinets, if only because I was getting embarrassed when my friends came over and saw I had nothing. "I only have vodka; I'm such a mess lol" is only cute for like two weeks.

I went to the cheapest section of Target, wistfully looked at a few cookie sheets, and patiently waited for someone to come over and do everything for me. They didn't, so I called my dad, hoping he might. I asked him what kind of pan we used to make the pork chops we ate every Sunday night when I was growing up. These were the only things I knew how to cook at this point, so I figured I'd start there. The idea of making these pork chops alone at home reminded me of a new neurosis and I started to cry.

Wasn't buying all this stuff supposed to be something you did with your spouse? Why did I have to do it all alone? Was something wrong with me? Would I be alone forever? Why didn't I get a roommate? Why did I have to find the cheap studio alone? Was I some sort of antisocial weirdo? Was I going to get *Taken*-ed, or *Taken 4*–ed, or *Taken*-the-TV-show-ed? You see, my singledom was another reality thing these pans represented that I didn't want to deal with. Not only was I an adult, but I was an adult on my own.

I relayed all these thoughts to my father and he happily told me that I was being a hysterical narcissist. I needed to stop thinking of myself as a character in a movie, he said. "This is what people do," he continued. "They buy things to start their lives! You do it alone and then you may do it again with someone else! Do you want to be independent or do you want to be a child? Do you want to wallow or be productive? You want to cook or not?" I wanted to cook, but I also definitely wanted to wallow and be a child. Wasn't that pretty fucking obvious, Dad? That's like my whole deal.

So after I calmed down, my father and I went over what to buy for the pork chops, and then a couple of other pots and pans and knives and doodads that I'd probably need, including a fabulous wine opener. When I asked him "Which white bowls for cereal?" he hung up. My dad will only indulge me so much. It's really lame.

Having purchased the necessary kitchen tools, I got home and put everything away. Then, with a new sense of confidence, I went to the supermarket and stocked my fridge and pantry. I finally bought salt. Going six months without salt because you are just that afraid of committing to yourself is not a good space to be in.

That night, I looked around my apartment and felt better than I had in a while. These weren't the perfect things I'd eventually want in my perfect home, but they were fine for now, and I'd find a way to make them look cool on Instagram. (It's all about angles.) These pots and pans also didn't mean I would be alone forever, but they did mean I was making a commitment to myself and my life in the moment. So I wasn't Holly Golightly in *Breakfast at Tiffany's*. I was Miranda Berman in her life, and maybe that was even more romantic in its own way? It wasn't, but then I remembered Holly's ending wasn't so happy in the book version, and I felt better. I also felt basic for imagining myself as Audrey Hepburn.

So follow my lead, and buy your pots and pans and make your little house a little home. At the least, doing so will allow you to cook for yourself, and at the most, it will make your less-together friends feel bad about themselves when they come over.

See you when you come back from the store!

THE KITCHEN EQUIPMENT YOU ACTUALLY NEED

GLM

What, you thought you could still get away with the two plastic bowls, microwave, and minifridge you had in your college dorm room? In short, no, but don't worry—outfitting your kitchen isn't as overwhelming as you might think!

KNIVES. Want to know a secret? Roughly 50 percent of the single-use kitchen gadgets on the market can be replaced by just one item: a good knife. It's also the tool you'll reach for most often. For these reasons, it's important to be choosy about your knives. The two most important knives in your arsenal are a good-quality chef's knife to tackle bigger jobs, like chopping vegetables and slicing meat, and a paring knife for little things, like cheese and small fruits. A good knife should feel comfortable in your hand. If you're buying your first knife, it's fine to get a simpler, less expensive one, just get it sharpened at least once a year (many kitchen supply stores will do this for free).

CUTTING BOARD. We recommend getting two or three cutting boards, in varying sizes (usually 13 × 9.5 inches, 11 × 8.5 inches, and 8 × 6 inches). Ideally, one of them should be wooden (bonus: a nice wooden cutting board can double as a serving platter for cooked meats or cheeses, bread, and fruit), and the other one or two should be plastic. Plastic cutting boards are usually cheaper and easier to

clean, so if your funds are limited, start with a couple of those.

TOOLS. Must-haves: a vegetable peeler, a hand-operated can opener (don't waste your money on an electric one; they're absurd—plus, how lazy can you be?), and two pairs of metal tongs (small ones and larger ones, which are great for grilling).

MIXING BOWLS. After a sharp chef's knife, mixing bowls are likely to be the most-used items in your kitchen. Between batter mixing and meat marinating and egg whipping and the occasional cereal binge, everything will go in bowls. Do yourself a favor and buy a set. Oh, and also, you can use them for serving! If you can find ones with matching lids (Pyrex makes a great version), storing your leftovers will be a snap, and potluck schlepping will be a lot easier (and less messy).

MEASURING CUPS. You need at least two sets: one for liquids (usually in tempered glass with a spout—the most common brand is Pyrex, with red lettering) and one for dry ingredients (usually cup-shaped with individual cups for each amount, designed to be filled and leveled off with a finger or knife). But if you only have space (or money) for one, get a glass one with a spout.

MEASURING SPOONS. You only need one set of measuring spoons. Don't bother with adorable ceramic ones from fancy boutiques—their cuteness will not be adequately appreciated (and you will absolutely break one when you drop it in the sink or on the floor). Opt instead for sturdy ones attached to a ring and make sure they have half measurements.

COLANDER. You've probably already used a colander to drain pasta, but it's a tool of many uses: draining cooked vegetables, rinsing salad greens, and steaming vegetables over simmering water. Don't bother with dinky plastic ones (they will fall apart and you can't use them for steaming); opt for a sturdy metal colander instead. If you can, get both a medium one (for small pots of pasta and vegetables) and a large one (which can be used to store fruit in the refrigerator until you need it to drain the fourteen potatoes you are mashing for Thanksgiving).

SPATULA. Get at least one, and make sure it's plastic (more flexible and won't damage nonstick cookware) and slotted (which helps drain excess oil and liquids from your food when transferring). You'll use it constantly.

NONSTICK SAUCEPAN. We recommend a 2-quart nonstick pot with comfortable handles (look for the kind with rubberized or plastic handles, designed to stay cooler during cooking). Great for soups, stews, and braising (make sure it's ovenproof).

NONSTICK OR CERAMIC FRYING PAN. You need at least one 8-inch pan, though adding a 12-inch one is even better (sometimes they come in sets, which can be a bargain). You'll sauté and pan-fry on a regular basis, and nonstick cookware is the easiest to clean. (Plus, how else are you supposed to scrape off those delicious cheese crispies that come from making a grilled cheese sandwich or quesadilla?)

CAST IRON PAN. A 12-inch cast iron pan typically costs about $20 (the Lodge brand is pretty much the gold standard), and as long as you take care of it, it will last your entire life. Make sure to buy a "seasoned" cast iron pan. Not only does it make the juiciest roast chicken, the most crispy-edged pancakes, and the crustiest baked mac and cheese, it also looks striking when you serve food in it. Just promise us you'll never use soap on it, and that you'll keep it lightly oiled.

RIMMED BAKING SHEET. Skip flat "cookie sheets" and go instead for rimmed ones. Rimmed baking sheets can certainly be used for cookie baking, but they are also amazing for just about anything that can be baked or roasted—plus their handy rims prevent spillage during cooking. We use them to roast vegetables, chicken legs, and potatoes on an almost weekly basis.

BAKING DISHES. Like mixing bowls, baking dishes do double duty by serving as the vessel for both cooking and, well, serving. Just about any baked casserole-type dish (think mac and cheese, lasagna, and enchiladas) needs to be made in a baking dish. Ultimately, you'll want to have a few: one or two pretty ones, and one or two tempered glass ones with matching lids (again, great for packing up leftovers and bringing dishes to parties). If you're just getting started with your cookware collection, get the tempered glass ones (ideally a large one, 11 × 17 inches, and a smaller one, 9 × 13 inches).

KITCHEN TOWELS. You'll use these for wiping up messes, covering dough that needs to rise, and protecting your hands from hot pans when your potholders are too far away. They're also a great way to give your kitchen a little bit of fun color, but don't spend too much on them! You'll likely go through them regularly, so buy a bunch at once. Wash them at least once a week to keep them from smelling like mildew.

POTHOLDERS AND OVEN MITTS. If you are anything like us, you'll only use potholders occasionally, when you remember to get them out. Most times you'll use the kitchen towels described above to handle hot pots and pans. But potholders are still worth having on hand, if only to act as impromptu trivets and to hang on the back of your pantry door to make your kitchen look like someone who cooks delicious food lives in your house (she does!). There are fancy silicone potholders and gloves, which will make you look like a futuristic *Top Chef* contestant, but regular cotton ones work just fine, are cheaper, and look cuter.

DISHWARE. Now that you're cooking, you're going to need some plates! Our two strongest recommendations are to head to Target, Bed Bath & Beyond, or a similar store and buy a cute but affordable set for at least four (which should include, at the very least, large dinner plates, smaller salad plates, and bowls), or to go to your local Goodwill or Salvation Army, where you can often find entire dishware sets, frequently from fancy-ass designers, for pennies per piece. Or, if you're a mix-and-matcher, you can put together an eclectic combination of dishes that will make you look like you live in an Anthropologie.

FLATWARE. Your approach to buying flatware can mimic (and be done at the same time as) buying dishware. Either buy a set or go hunting for pieces. Just be sure you get at least four forks (one or two sizes), four teaspoons, four soup spoons, and four butter knives. If you're a big meat-eater, you may also want to consider getting four steak knives.

DRINKING GLASSES. Buy a combination of tall and shorter tumblers (tall for water and beer, short for cocktails and wine, if you don't have wineglasses). And yes, it's totally okay to buy a set or two of mason jars and use these. Glassware can be the window to the soul, so get fun colors to show how fun and funky your soul is.

STOCKING A PANTRY LIKE YOU KNOW WHAT YOU'RE DOING
GLM & MPB

Some things are just necessary to have. Like Netflix, deodorant, and a really fun person to flirt with at work. The same goes for a good pantry. Gabi's pantry was a little more stocked than Miranda's when we examined them side by side, but we came to the following list together and we're pretty pleased with it. In our experience, these are the shelf-stable items you'll return to over and over again.

We find that when we have these basics on hand, we need only to pick up a few fresh ingredients (fruit, vegetables, meat, fish, tofu, eggs, etc.) to put together a tasty, healthful, homemade meal in a snap. We usually buy pantry staples at Trader Joe's or from discount stores like Smart & Final or Costco, where we can get the best deals. Alternately, if your workplace stocks a fridge or pantry, steal from there. Just do it in small increments so your employers are none the wiser. Definitely steal toilet paper from work. That's obvious.

PANTRY STAPLES
- Unbleached all-purpose flour
- Extra-virgin olive oil (Be sure to always buy olive oil labeled "extra virgin," and buy something you enjoy the taste of. We're fond of Trader Joe's California Estate Olive Oil, which costs around $6 for a bottle and tastes like an Italian sunrise.)
- Neutral oil, like vegetable oil, canola oil, or coconut oil
- Kosher salt
- Black pepper (we like the kind that comes in a grinder)
- Baking soda
- Baking powder
- White granulated sugar
- Brown sugar
- Honey
- Balsamic vinegar
- Peanut butter (your favorite kind)
- Mayonnaise
- Whole garlic heads
- Yellow or white onions
- Dried pasta
- Canned beans
- Rice (white, brown, or both)
- Coffee beans (whole or ground, depending on your grinder situation)
- Tea (bagged or loose leaf, depending on your style)

DAMN, CHECK OUT THAT (SPICE) RACK

GLM

Spices are a little like designated drivers: you almost always need at least one of them at your disposal, but it can feel stupid to have a whole bunch of them hanging around. On one hand, most recipes call for just one or two of them—maybe three or four, but that's usually only if you're making a spice-centric dish like a chili or a curry. On the other hand, not having a spice you need can sometimes keep a whole dish from coming together (kind of like trying to get home from a party *without* a DD, which you should NEVER EVER do, obviously). Your best bet is to have a solid collection of spices and replenish or add to it as necessary. Oh, and FYI, spices do not last forever. Experts say you should replace them every six months. Personally, I think you can get away with once a year or so.

For the very best deals on spices, buy them in bulk or at Indian grocery stores, where they're sold in plastic packets. Transfer them to little mason jars and label them (if you're into that kind of thing). Otherwise, Whole Foods' 365 spice brand and Simply Organic are good and fairly affordable options.

Here are my picks for a full rack (and this kind of full rack comes sans the lower back pain!):

BAY LEAVES. Normally sold dried (fresh ones smell heavenly but are really too strong to use in cooking), bay leaves give a woodsy flavor to long-cooking foods like soups, chilies, and stews. They are typically sold as whole leaves and should be removed from the dish before serving (unless you like eating eucalyptus-tasting leaves, in which case, consult your doctor).

CAYENNE PEPPER. Cayenne pepper is the flavor base of most American hot sauces (think Crystal and Tabasco), and is a tasty way to add a hint of perky spice to food.

CHILI POWDER. When you buy standard chili powder, it's usually a blend of dried red chili peppers, cumin, coriander, and sometimes oregano. Ancho chili powder, however, and any other chili powder that indicates the chili species, is normally just straight ground chili pepper. We typically prefer the latter to the former, as it is usually a purer flavor. It's the virgin of chili powders, saving itself for Luke Perry.

CINNAMON, GROUND. You can't make cinnamon toast without it (and we have to make cinnamon toast), and it's a must on oatmeal,

but cinnamon can also be key in dishes you wouldn't necessarily guess, like chilies, curry, and soups.

CUMIN, GROUND. Often called for in Latin and Indian cooking, cumin has a deep, almost smoky flavor. It is also sold in seed form, but opt for the ground variety. The seeds are great for pickling, but unless you plan on doing a lot of that, choose the powdered kind. But, I mean, if you're the type who lives in Greenpoint and has a rooftop garden and a fixie bike, and you do a lot of pickling, by all means, get the seeds too.

CURRY POWDER. There are many different varieties of curry powder, which contains as many as twenty spices depending on the brand. It's the basis of many Indian sauces, but also a classic addition to chicken and egg salads.

NUTMEG, GROUND. Though nutmeg is often paired with cinnamon in warm, autumnal dishes, it's fabulous in its own right. It has the power to make foods like cheeses, pumpkin, and sweet potato taste more like themselves. But beware—a little goes a long way and it's easy to overwhelm a dish with nutmeg if you add too much.

OREGANO, DRIED. We're generally not huge fans of dried herbs (fresh ones are cheaper and taste better), but oregano is an exception. Because it's so intensely flavored, the drying process helps mellow it out to just the right strength. It's frequently used in Mexican, Greek, and Italian cooking.

PAPRIKA, SWEET AND SMOKED. Normally we wouldn't suggest you buy two varieties of the same thing, but sweet and smoked paprika are two vastly different spices. Sweet paprika is piquant and peppery—great to sprinkle over chicken before baking or atop deviled eggs. Smoked paprika, on the other hand, is intensely smoky and earthy. We think it makes food taste slightly bacon-y, especially when combined with brown sugar and black pepper. And who doesn't want everything to taste a little like bacon?

RED PEPPER FLAKES (AKA CHILI FLAKES, AKA CRUSHED RED PEPPER). These guys add heat and color to just about everything. We use them so often that we buy them in bulk, but if you don't, just ask for a few extra containers the next time you order a pizza, and hoard them; they're the same thing.

THYME, DRIED. Thyme is one more dried herb we think is a must-have. It's mildly flavored and slightly lemony—perfect for when you want to give a dish a little fresh, green flavor without overpowering it. We love it on roast chicken, in Greek dressings (it's magical with feta), and sprinkled over mac and cheese.

VANILLA EXTRACT. Good vanilla is necessary for many baking projects (and our vanilla latte recipe on page 121), so it's worth getting the good stuff (skip the imitation vanilla—you might as well be pouring mouthwash into your chocolate chip cookies). However, if you ever run out, dark rum can make an acceptable substitute for vanilla (but don't use it as mouthwash).

GROCERY SHOPPING ALONE CAN BE SEXY

GLM & MPB

Miranda was once buying a piece of fish for herself to cook, but at the last second she lied to the fishmonger and said she needed two pieces. She told herself she'd make the second piece the next night, but really she just liked how the fishmonger saw her in that moment. He probably thought she was going home to whip up a last-minute dinner for her novelist husband, or cool artist wife, or secret French lover. She wanted to play that part, even for an instant, even in someone else's mind.

Miranda didn't want to play the part of "Sad Woman Eating/Shopping Alone," which as a trope is far too popular in modern culture. Like its offshoots, "Woman Whose Shopping Basket Contains Only Cat Food" and "Woman Eating Häagen-Dazs on Couch While Crying," female solo dining implies that a heroine is recently dumped, depressed, and usually in need of a make-over montage. We're calling bullshit.

First of all, grocery shopping on your own can actually be sexy. Miranda shouldn't have been pretending to be married in the fish department. She should have been flirting in the beer aisle. Single people are always chilling at the grocery store after work. They, like you, saved dinner for the last minute and are picking something up. The meat market is a meat market; we're telling you. And second, cooking for yourself demonstrates nothing other than that you are a gorgeous, brilliant, independent woman who knows how to feed her hunger. And part of feeding yourself, as you well know, is shopping for yourself.

These are the items that fill our usual healthy grocery basket. (Okay, there's usually ice cream and we do occasionally eat it alone on the couch.) We suggest trying it our way, then editing it to meet your needs.

———————————————————————

PRODUCE

GREENS. Those you can eat cooked or raw, like baby spinach or kale (go for dark-green dinosaur/lacinato kale as opposed to the lighter-green curly variety). Use them to make salads or sauté in a bit of olive oil for a quick, healthy side dish.

SNACK VEGETABLES. Baby carrots, mini Persian cucumbers, mini bell peppers, or any other crunchy, easy-to-eat-raw vegetable. These are great for healthy snacking and can also be used in cooking.

1 OR 2 MEDIUM ONIONS. We usually buy yellow ones (which we find have the most flavor), but white or red are okay too. Look for what's on sale.

1 HEAD OF GARLIC. You can also totally buy packages of whole peeled cloves—just be sure you use them promptly, since they're going to get slimy and weird smelling in a week or so. But do not (we repeat, DO NOT) buy the chopped, jarred variety; it doesn't taste as good, and it's more expensive than fresh.

FRESH HERBS. Using fresh herbs is the quickest way to take your cooking from average to great with very little effort. Our weekly buys are cilantro for Asian/Latin dishes and flat-leaf parsley for Italian/Mediterranean. Mint and basil are semiregulars (especially in the summer). Always buy a full bunch as opposed to the measly little plastic boxes that contain like seven leaves and cost $6.

1 OR 2 LEMONS. Even if we don't use them in cooking, we're always squeezing them into water or booze. Plus, they look pretty in a bowl on the counter.

FRUIT. Apples, oranges, bananas, or another in-season, easy-to-eat fruit. If it's easy to eat and requires little to no prep beyond washing, you are more likely to eat it, which is the idea.

1 OR 2 AVOCADOS. We know avocado toast is kind of basic, but there's no denying it's so good. Plus, avocados make every salad, taco, and tortilla chip taste way better. Here's the trick: If you think you'll eat two in a week, buy one that is ripe and one that is still a little hard. The hard one will be ripe by the time you're ready to use it.

GRAPES. Sure, they're good with cheese, but we have a better plan: Rinse and put them in the freezer until they harden. You'll have a healthy dessert option on hand for when late-night cravings for sweets hit. They're like magical little bites of sorbet.

EGGS AND DAIRY

1 DOZEN EGGS. Great for breakfast on a toasted English muffin (check out page 128 for our spin on the egg sando), but also just an excellent source of high-quality protein. There is so much you can do with eggs. Hard- or soft-boil a few and keep them around as a nutritious snack, or chop them up and put them over salad greens.

HALF-AND-HALF. Half-and-half is for so much more than coffee. You can use it to thicken creamy soups, sauces, and curries, but you can also dilute it with water—use equal parts half-and-half and water—to make milk. (We know

it seems weird, but it totally works.) We don't drink straight milk, so we keep half-and-half around for when we need it for cereal or a recipe calling for milk.

CHEESE. Choose something with mild flavor that can be used for a variety of things, including snacking on. Low-moisture mozzarella, mild or medium cheddar, and jack are all good options. Use it in sandwiches, shredded over scrambled eggs, cubed in salad, or stirred into pasta.

BUTTER. We usually buy two kinds: unsalted, for cooking and baking with, and salted, for spreading on bread, corn, oatmeal, and anything else you'd put butter on (everything, but we know we shouldn't).

MEAT/FISH/TOFU

Here are some favorites. We usually buy one or two per week.

SAUSAGES. Buy them at the meat counter, not prepackaged. They'll be fresher and cheaper, and you can buy only the amount you need (we usually get them in pairs).

VEGETARIAN SAUSAGES. Our favorite brands include Tofurky and Field Roast.

WHOLE CHICKEN LEGS. (See page 41 for our favorite way to serve them.)

GROUND BEEF. (For chili and burgers—see page 253 for our favorite chili and 249 for our badass burger recipe.)

CLEANED, DEVEINED SHRIMP. They cook super fast and are packed with protein. Lovely atop a salad or with risotto (see page 63).

EXTRA-FIRM SPROUTED TOFU. The sprouted variety is generally the firmest, and therefore easiest to cook without worrying about crumbling. (See page 51 for the way we make it.)

HOW TO GET OUT OF WHOLE FOODS WITHOUT DIPPING INTO YOUR 401(K)

GLM & MPB

We'll admit it: We love Whole Foods. The stores are clean and pleasant to shop in; the salespeople are generally knowledgeable and helpful; the produce is beautiful and often locally sourced. The meat and seafood departments are impeccable. And you can usually find some sort of natural equivalent of Xanax or painkillers. It's honestly the Neiman Marcus of supermarkets, and it makes us feel fancy . . . maybe too fancy?

Yes, Whole Foods is notorious for being crazy expensive (Whole Paycheck, anyone?), but we've found that with a little bit of planning and insight, it is indeed possible to complete a Whole Foods shop without bankrupting oneself. This is how.

SHOP MOSTLY ON THE OUTSIDE AISLES. In most Whole Foods stores, the outside aisles contain the bulk section, the produce section, the meat and seafood counters, and the dairy and egg refrigerator cases. In our experience, these are the best things to shop for at Whole Foods. Not only do they tend to be the healthiest items in the store, but also you generally find the most selection (and often very good sales!) in these departments. The prepared, processed, and packaged foods tend to be the higher-ticket items. And it should go without saying that while it's cool that Whole Foods sells yoga mats and $40 water bottles, you (and your grocery budget) do not need them.

AT THE MEAT AND SEAFOOD DEPARTMENTS, GO WITH THE CHEAPER ITEMS. Whole Foods has very high standards for all its products, so even the least expensive cuts of meat and seafood are very high quality. Opt for chicken legs over breasts, and sirloin, flank, and skirt steaks over the New York strip. Get the sole over the swordfish. And while you're in the meat and seafood department . . .

ASK THE BUTCHERS AND FISHMONGERS TO HELP YOU OUT. In addition to being knowledgeable about the products they sell, the people behind the meat and seafood counters are the ones who clean, debone, skin, fillet, grind, and trim the proteins. Don't be shy about asking them to do some of the prep work for you. If whole fish are on sale, buy them (they're much cheaper per pound than skinned, precut fish fillets or steaks), and have the fishmonger clean, skin, and fillet them for you, free of charge.

BUY IN-SEASON PRODUCE FOR THE BEST PRICES. There's a simple reason why a locally grown tomato in July costs less than a flown-in-from-Chile tomato in January: airfare. When we buy fruits and vegetables grown near where we live (which is only possible when they're in season), they cost less because the produce doesn't have to travel as far. Whole Foods generally has most of its produce available year-round (often flown in), but it also works with many local farms to bring in the best of what's in season.

LEARN TO LOVE THE BULK SECTION. Some of the best deals at Whole Foods can be found in these bins. When you buy in bulk, you are paying for only the food itself, not packaging, so the price is significantly lower than that of prepackaged goods. It's great for when you need a lot of something, but it's also wonderful for when you need only a little. (Why buy a 24-ounce package of walnuts when you only need a quarter cup of them for a recipe?) It's worth the annoying twelve seconds it takes to wrap a twist-tie around a plastic bag and write the product code on it. Invest in a pack of cheap jumbo-size mason jars to store things like flour, sugar, rice, beans, pasta, oats, nuts, and dried fruit from the bulk section. Putting them in an airtight container like a mason jar will keep them fresh longer. And it looks adorable.

SHOP LIKE A EUROPEAN. We know this isn't possible for everyone. When you have a nine-to-five job and children and errands, it can be hard to regularly practice the classic European way of shopping, which is to keep a pantry stocked with basic nonperishables and then augment a few times a week with small quantities of fresh items: a piece of meat or fish here, some cheese and eggs there, and whichever fruits and vegetables are gorgeous and seasonal. It means more stops at the store, but when you can, this is one of the most cost-effective ways to shop. Since it requires you to grocery shop on an as-needed basis (as opposed to the more traditional American style of filling a cart with enough food for two weeks), you are far more likely to actually use all of what you buy. (How many times has the lettuce you optimistically bought a week ago been left to turn to mush in your crisper because you never got around to eating it?) Nothing is sadder than a compost bin drawer full of never-used produce gone bad!

REMEMBER, THESE PRINCIPLES CAN BE APPLIED TO OTHER SUPERMARKETS AND HEALTH FOOD STORES TOO. Whole Foods is obviously the most ubiquitous whole food grocer in the country, but, if you're lucky, there are other good options available where you live as well. Remember: Just because a store is generally expensive doesn't mean it has to be off-limits. A little careful planning and a discerning eye can help you stock your kitchen with healthful real food without giving you cause to declare bankruptcy. And whatever you do, don't forget your reusable bags, lest you suffer the epic shade-throwing by judgmental cashiers.

THE ART OF CLEANING AS YOU COOK

GLM & MPB

Part of what makes cooking so daunting is that you have to clean up afterward, and cleaning is terrible. It's only fun when you're having an emotional breakdown and can't concentrate on anything else, or if you're Monica Geller. Cleaning as you cook will stop you from feeling overwhelmed, and is really the opposite of hot mess behavior. It might very well turn you into a full-fledged normal adult overnight. Gabi converted Miranda. And we're telling you: Cleaning as you cook will literally solve all your problems. Literally, all of them.

We know this sounds like a boring section you want to skip over, but it's actually hella useful. We put it in the book because we want to set you up for success. We hear being set up for success is a thing. And honestly, not everyone knows how to clean well. Some of us need cleaning lessons. Don't be ashamed if you've never cleaned before, if you're a total pig living in squalor. Don't be ashamed, but now it's time to change. Clean as though the love of your life is on their way over.

START WITH A CLEAN KITCHEN. This seems obvious, but how many times have you gone into the kitchen to cook and found a mess (courtesy of roommates, or of the midnight snack you had the night before)? It's much easier to keep a kitchen clean when you're only managing the mess made from the recipe you're currently working on. Take ten minutes to wash last night's dishes, wipe down the counters, and clear the drying rack or unload the dishwasher so you don't have to deal with dish spillover later on.

FILL THE SINK WITH WARM, SOAPY WATER AND PUT DISHES AND UTENSILS IN IT AS YOU FINISH WITH THEM. When you're done, you'll have a sink full of nearly clean dishes that likely need little more than a quick wipe and a rinse to be fully clean. The warm water and soap will also help to soften any cooked-on yuck. And there's always some yuck. Get some kind of moisturizing dish soap. This will leave your hands feeling beautiful and soft like a queen's. Or you can buy some hilarious dishwashing gloves.

IF FOOD FALLS ON THE FLOOR WHILE YOU'RE COOKING, PICK IT UP IMMEDIATELY. You CAN and probably SHOULD eat it. It's a little floor amuse-bouche for you. Not only does food on the floor get grosser and harder to clean up every time you step on it, but it can be a banana-peel gag waiting to happen, so unless one of your guests is your mortal enemy and you want them to fall to their death in your kitchen, you should pick up the food. You'll give the floor a good sweeping and mopping after cooking, but give yourself a head start by keeping the floor free of sizable food bits.

KEEP THE TRASH CAN (AND COMPOST BIN, IF YOU HAVE ONE) CLOSE TO YOUR WORKSTATION. When you're prepping something that will result in food scraps, like peeling an onion, it's easier to clear your space of scraps when the garbage or compost is nearby. If you keep it under the sink or in a corner, pull it over to where you are. Even better, use a countertop compost bin or garbage bowl and transfer waste into it frequently. And make

sure to empty the trash regularly—your vegetable scraps and chicken necks won't fit in the garbage if it's filled to the brim with your ex-boyfriend's stupid fraternity T-shirt collection and all your unpaid parking tickets. (Also: Pay those. You know the price goes up over time, right?)

MEASURE MESSY INGREDIENTS OVER THE SINK. Sticky liquids like honey or maple syrup or greasy ones like oil and butter are extremely annoying to clean off of countertops. The solution? Measure them over the sink. If you spill a little, just turn on the faucet and send it down the drain.

WHEN YOU'RE DOING BIG COOKING PROJECTS, TRY TO STOP EVERY TWENTY MINUTES OR SO TO TIDY UP. Look for breaks in recipes, like when water is boiling or the oven is preheating, to do a little cleanup. Though it may be tempting to use this time to drink cooking wine and drunk-sext your friend with benefits / cute work crush / favorite summer camp counselor, trust us when we say your time is better used wiping down counters and stovetops. For lots of reasons. Come on.

WHAT ACTUALLY CAN'T GO IN THE DISHWASHER

GLM

I f you are lucky enough to have a dishwasher, first of all, yay for you! The rest of you poor (probably apartment-dwelling) plebes can skip to the next section. Dishwashers are great. They're a huge time-saver for cleanup, and also a great way to give yourself a spa-like facial without leaving your house (just open it up midcycle and *aaahhhh!*). Your mother probably yelled at you for putting wooden spoons in the dishwasher when you were a teenager, just trying to rush through the dishes so you could finish your homework / stare at and pretend to make out with the *NSync poster in your room, but here is the real deal about what cannot go in the dishwasher. Consider everything else fair game. Even fish. (Seriously. Google it.)

CAST IRON. Not only should it never enter your dishwasher, but cast iron shouldn't even be washed with soap (weird, we know, but trust us). To clean cast iron, wash it by hand using a sponge or stiff brush under hot running water, just until all the debris has been removed. Then rub in a little olive or vegetable oil with a paper towel, just to thinly coat the surface, kind of like how you always apply sunscreen, instead of how you're actually supposed to slather it on in a thick layer.

SHARP KNIVES. Butter knives are fine. Anything sharper than that will get dull in the dishwasher, so wash it by hand.

CRYSTAL. First of all, you own crystal? You may be too fancy for this book. But in any case, hand-wash it. But you probably already knew that, seeing as you own crystal.

WOODEN UTENSILS. Super-hot water and dish detergent can soften wood over time and wear off any sealants on it, causing it to break down quickly. Best to hand-wash and air-dry.

NONSTICK POTS AND PANS. The dishwasher process can remove the nonstick coating, which is the whole reason you bought those pots and pans in the first place. Plus, pots and pans take up half of a dishwashing rack, so you're saving the earth by scrubbing them in the sink, rinsing, and either towel- or air-drying (we live in California, give us the water).

ANYTHING WITH A LABEL. We know it can seem like a good idea to put that old pickle jar in the dishwasher to remove the adhesive so you can turn it into a rustic hipster vase, but the adhesives will just wash away and clog up the dishwasher drain. Instead, try rubbing it with a little olive oil to break up the label glue residue, and then scrubbing it under hot water.

Did you read the intro? Promise? This wasn't like an annoying intro to a book in high school. It was useful information! You did? Swear? Didn't skip over? (It's okay if you did.) Do you have pans and produce and a sexy spice rack? Now you are ready to start cooking. We're kind of excited for you. It's like when your best friend tells you she just lost her virginity and you get secondhand excitement, or you just get jealous because you're a late bloomer. It's like, *Get pumped. You're in for so much fun.*

CHAPTER 1

Broke AF

Being broke is a blessing.

I know it's hard to believe (especially if you're reading this while eating cheese out of a can on generic-brand Triscuits in your freezing-cold box-size apartment, where your toilet is in your kitchen), but I promise you, it's true. First of all, you are probably broke for a series of good reasons: you're climbing the rungs of your dream career, and those low rungs don't pay well; you spent a shitload of money on college or grad school and now you have to pay the government (or your parents) back while climbing said low rungs; you're living in a fabulous, exciting city where rent costs more than the gross national product of some small countries; you're still learning how to manage money, and, like most people, you're finding it's not easy. I get it. I've been there. In some ways, I'm still there.

But being broke or near-broke lights an essential fire under you. You know the fear and anxiety that is not being sure how you'll manage to pay your rent. It means dreading the potential of having to ask your parents or friends to lend you some cash. And that anxiety, while temporarily paralyzing, pushes you to avoid such outcomes. While making more money may not be an immediately available option, spending less always is. And the first step to take when you want to spend less is to stop going out or ordering in for every meal and learn to cook at home.

Cooking at home doesn't mean trading dinner at that fabulous new tapas joint for a sad, generic-brand can of soup. Nor does it mean slaving over a hot stove when you come home from work at 8 p.m. In this chapter, we do our best to show you how to make simple, easy, very inexpensive meals that won't leave you missing the restaurant experience.

Of course, if you're really missing the *true* restaurant experience, you can always make yourself wait forty-five minutes before you sit down at your table and set up an awkward coed handwashing station outside your bathroom. —GLM

SOMEDAY I'LL BE RICH RICE AND BEANS

GLM

Combining rice and beans has been a cheap, nutritious solution to hunger for as long as men have been lying about their height (read: since the dawn of time / the Fertile Crescent). From Southern red beans and rice to black or pinto beans and rice, served all over South and Central America, the combo is a good way to satisfy hunger without spending a lot of money. Even better, when beans and rice come together, they form a complete protein. We're not entirely sure what this means, but we know it's a good thing.

This combination of good ol' beans and rice is a riff on everyone's favorite Chipotle option, the burrito bowl: a scrumptious medley that combines all your favorite burrito fillings (rice, beans, veggies, cheese, minus an annoying reminder that "guac is extra"). It's filling, thanks to the fiber and protein in the beans and rice, and crazy flavorful, thanks to the veggies and garlic.

We love this recipe on its own, right out of the bowl, but we've also been known to spoon it over chips, top with shredded cheese, and broil for two to three minutes for loaded, vaguely healthy nachos, or to stuff it into warm corn tortillas for what is basically the best vegetarian taco out there.

Life is crazy, guys. Be your own Chipotle.

INGREDIENTS

2 tablespoons extra-virgin olive oil

1 large carrot, diced

1 clove garlic, minced

½ cup frozen green peas

¼ white onion, diced

½ cup uncooked long-grain brown rice

Pinch of salt

½ (15-ounce) can black beans, drained and rinsed

1 handful fresh cilantro leaves, roughly chopped

Optional toppings: sour cream; guacamole or avocado; leftover cooked chicken, beef, or tofu

DIRECTIONS

- In a large pot, heat the oil over medium heat.

- Add the carrots, garlic, peas, and three-quarters of the diced onion. Cook, stirring occasionally, until the onions are translucent.

- Add the rice, stir well, and cook for 1 minute.

- Stir in 1 cup of water and the salt.

- Cover and reduce heat to low. Allow to cook for 20 minutes.

- Meanwhile, heat the beans and ½ cup of water in a pot over medium heat or in the microwave, until heated through. Drain the beans before serving.

- Once the rice is cooked and the beans are hot, transfer both to a serving bowl.

- Top with the reserved diced onion and the cilantro, plus any of the optional toppings you like.

SERVES 1

ONE WEEK TILL PAYDAY PASTA

GLM

We've all been there.

You always start out with such responsible intentions. You deposit your paycheck on a Friday afternoon and *totally* don't spend it all at the bar. For the first week of the pay period, you are a glowing example of frugality, waking early enough to have coffee at home and catch the bus to work. You cook healthful, inexpensive meals, divide them into Tupperware containers, and eat them for lunch every day. You paint your nails yourself instead of splurging on gel manicures (they look terrible, but you just tell everyone your niece did them).

You are gonna do it, you promise yourself. You are gonna make that paycheck last the whole month.

But then the dreaded unexpected expense arises. Maybe your hot neighbor Mike invites you to join him and his equally cute friends for happy hour, and, wanting to impress him, you offer to pick up the tab, not realizing that his hot but pretentious friend Nick ordered a Johnnie Walker Blue Label that cost $27. But whatevs, you're a little tipsy, and you're feeling generous.

Then, of course, you're a little too drunk to take the train home, so you hail a cab. Oh, and you can't go to bed without stopping for pizza, so you ask the cabbie to pick up a slice. There's a line at the pizza place, and your cab meter is still running, but you *need* pizza.

The next day, you obviously oversleep, are running late, and dash out the door with still-wet hair. You run to a café to get a muffin, hoping it will settle your stomach. You wash it down with a triple-shot venti latte, grab a Lyft to save time, and barely make it to work before nine. Suddenly, three weeks of compensatory spending have passed and you have about $0.12 to your name. And yet, you still have to eat.

This pasta, which is made entirely from pantry ingredients (yes, you can use the shelf-stable Parmesan that comes in the can, but you can also skip it), is your key to survival. It's crazy flavorful, thanks to the garlic and red pepper flakes, and it has a fabulous crunch, thanks to the bread crumbs.

ONE WEEK TILL PAYDAY PASTA

INGREDIENTS

8 ounces dried spaghetti or other long-strand pasta

3 tablespoons extra-virgin olive oil

3 cloves garlic, chopped, or 1 tablespoon dried garlic granules

½ cup bread crumbs

2 teaspoons red pepper flakes

⅛ cup grated Parmesan (optional)

1 handful fresh parsley, chopped (optional)

Salt and pepper

NOTE: If you don't have bread crumbs, find any plain bread item in your cupboard (pitas, hot dog buns—even crackers will do) and either chop them or pulse them in a food processor until finely processed.

DIRECTIONS

• Cook the pasta in salted boiling water according to package directions.

• While the pasta cooks, heat the oil in a medium-size frying pan over medium-high heat.

• Add the garlic and cook for about 1 minute, stirring frequently to avoid burning.

• Add the bread crumbs and stir to combine well with garlic and oil.

• Allow the crumbs to toast for a few minutes, stirring occasionally.

• When the pasta has finished cooking, drain it and return it to its pot.

• Toss the bread crumb mixture, red pepper flakes, Parmesan, and parsley with the pasta. Season with salt and pepper to taste.

SERVES 2

BOUNCED CHECK BURRITO

MPB

Let's talk about overspending!

I have been totally broke for plenty of different reasons: the relatable reason of being unemployed, and the entirely unrelatable reason of shopping too much. The latter is the one I'll be discussing today. If I made a little money, I'd spend it. That movie *Confessions of a Shopaholic* is a biting drama and should have won an Oscar. Basically, shopping is my Xanax. Xanax is also my Xanax. Shopping on Xanax is my heroin. All this is to say that I am base-level fiscally irresponsible. I once got out of jury duty by flat-out saying, "I don't understand how money works." I dropped economics twice in college. I couldn't pay attention to the class, just like I can't pay attention to my own money, or rather I didn't want to pay attention to my own money. And for a while I didn't have to.

I had a very good mafia-style scheme working for me. I would write my rent check and then immediately go buy groceries for the week. The next day, the check would be cashed and I would go into overdraft for somewhere between twenty and forty-eight hours. I would spend no money during that time and it would be okay. Sure, I hadn't gone even a month without being in overdraft, but I was eating and I had a place to live. Having bad credit was, to me, well worth living beyond my means. (Credit? What's credit? Go buy *Finance for Dummies*. This is a cookbook.)

This was a bad plan.

Once, I was paying for my groceries at my local market when my credit card was declined. I didn't believe it; there must have been something wrong with the machine. My plan was foolproof and also really smart and interesting. There was a line behind me and people were starting to get antsy, hissing and yelling slurs. Your basic Slytherin stuff. I begged the checkout girl to put everything aside and promised to come right back with another card. I'm a master at making salespeople feel sorry for me.

I went to the ATM, checked my account, and realized I was in overdraft and my plan had failed. I tried to take out cash anyway. Then I tried to take out cash from a three-year-old unemployment debit card I'd received in the mail. I didn't want to believe it had come to this. Neither worked. There was also no other card. Given my terrible credit, I'd been denied an application for a credit card four times.

I got home, groceryless, only to find a note from my landlord. My rent check had also bounced, for the second month in a row. I called my bank. My account had been temporarily shut down and they were no longer willing to cover me. Since I'm often one to jump to terrible conclusions, to me, this meant the end of the world. It was a sign from the universe that I was unable to live on my own and would have to go into a rehab clinic for irresponsible entitled dumbasses. (Actually, I want to go there. But I can't afford it.) Sadly, I couldn't just jump to hysterics. I would have to pay my rent. So I used my histrionics to cry to my landlord. She sent me to the Russian owner of my building. Uncomfortable, he sent me to his wife. In tears, I begged her to give me more time. They gave me three weeks and I finally used three weeks' worth of paychecks to cover my rent, plus the late fee. I also used my tears to go to the accounting department at work and ask for a month's advance pay. (I know they say you shouldn't cry at work, but sometimes you have to!)

There was a caveat, though. From that point on, I would have to pay my rent in cash. This meant absolutely no fun *Ocean's Eleven*–style plan. It meant full responsibility and paying attention to my finances. Being boring and realizing that I had to take control of my life. Balancing my checkbook and whatnot. So I would have to find a new, responsible way of eating and spending my money. This burrito is that way. This could also be your Balancing Your Checkbook Burrito, 'cause that's what I do while eating it.

I am aware that this story is not *that* bad. It's more a story about avoiding things than anything else, but that's what I've been known to be good at. Unfortunately, when it comes to your finances, you can't avoid them. You have to deal with them if you want a place to live, food to eat, and a credit score that will get you a credit card, which at the time of publishing this book I was finally able to do. I'm sure it will be taken away from me any day, though.

NOTE: We typically eat one of these right after we make it and freeze a second one to be microwaved later. You can also make a big batch and freeze them all, ensuring you are never without a hot, delicious burrito. To freeze, simply wrap the burrito in a paper towel or two and then tightly in aluminum foil, and stick it in the freezer. To heat, remove the foil and microwave the paper-towel-wrapped burrito on a microwave-safe plate for 2½ to 3 minutes, until heated through.

BOUNCED CHECK BURRITO

INGREDIENTS

½ cup uncooked long-grain white or brown rice

1 clove garlic, minced

1 teaspoon chili powder

¼ teaspoon salt, plus a pinch

¼ teaspoon pepper

1 (15-ounce) can black beans, drained and rinsed

2 large flour tortillas

¼ cup grated jack cheese

½ avocado, sliced

1 small tomato, chopped

¼ white onion, finely chopped

1 small bunch cilantro, finely chopped

¼ cup sour cream

Hot sauce (optional)

DIRECTIONS

- Combine the rice with 1 cup water, the garlic, the chili powder, and ¼ teaspoon each of salt and pepper in a small pot over high heat.

- Bring to a boil, then reduce to a simmer and cook, covered, for 20 minutes, or until fully cooked. Fluff with a fork and set aside.

- Meanwhile, heat the beans in a small saucepan with 2 tablespoons water. Add the pinch of salt and stir to incorporate. Set aside.

- To prepare each burrito, lay a tortilla on a flat surface and add a sprinkle of the cheese. Top with ½ cup cooked rice, ½ cup black beans, a few slices of avocado, and 2 tablespoons each of chopped tomato, onions, cilantro, and sour cream.

- Roll the tortilla tightly, making sure to tuck in the ends first.

- Heat a large, dry frying pan over high heat. Cook the rolled burrito for 1 to 2 minutes on each side to sear lightly. Cut in half and serve with hot sauce, if desired.

SERVES 2

THE CHICEST TV DINNER YOU EVER SAW

GLM & MPB

All that we've ever wanted for this book is for it to inspire you to stop buying frozen meals. To bid adieu to shrink-wrapped frozen burritos, low-fat lasagnas, and anything else that requires you to poke holes in a layer of cellophane before nuking it into oblivion. But look, we're realists, and we know that sometimes you are just too hungry and too tired to make something from scratch. Frozen meals are cheap, and we also totally get their appeal as take-to-work lunches—sometimes you just can't be bothered to pack something you're going to be interested in eating. And so Smart Ones, Lean Cuisine, and Amy's make their way into your grocery basket. And stay in your freezer for nights when you're super desperate. We get it.

On their own, they're okay. But here's a little hot mess magic to make them pretty damn good.

THE CHICEST TV DINNER YOU EVER SAW

SEASON THEM TO YOUR LIKING.

Frozen meals typically come plenty salty (often with too much salt), so steer away from adding more sodium to them. Think instead of fresh herbs: those Amy's enchiladas will be even tastier if you add some fresh sliced green onions and cilantro to them, and that lasagna will taste more Italian with some freshly snipped basil. We also love adding hot sauces, fresh lemon or lime juice, and plenty of black pepper to our frozen foods.

PUT THEM ON AN ACTUAL PLATE OR IN A BOWL.

After microwaving, use a spoon or scraper spatula to transfer your meal onto a real plate or bowl. Pour a glass of wine or sparkling water, and treat your meal (even if it's in the break room at work or at your desk) like an actual meal. It'll taste better, we promise.

ADD A FRESH VEGETABLE OF SOME KIND.

A crisp green salad, slaw, or even raw carrot sticks. The extra fiber will make you feel more full, and the whole meal experience will be improved by the added freshness.

CHEAP CHICKEN LEGS (AND A FREE TRIP TO EUROPE)

MPB

have huge gossip for you.

I like chicken legs better than chicken breasts. Yes, it's true. The legs are juicer, they have more flavor, they have more fat (mmmmmm, fat), and you can buy them whole for a fraction of the cost of breasts. In fact, this chicken legs recipe is my go-to for whenever I don't know what to eat. I've made it for friends, dates, and myself.

Actually, I like eating these chicken legs best when I'm alone at home with nothing to do. They make me feel French. There's nothing particularly French about this recipe, but it reminds me of this chicken dish I order at my favorite French bistro in LA.

This meal then allows me to escape my life for a hot second and pretend I live in Paris. I put on my caftan, I pour myself a glass of inexpensive or stolen pinot noir.* (You can also use water with red food coloring or grape juice. This is a fantasy.) I play some Édith Piaf, *et voilà*, I am no longer Miranda. I am *Mee-ran-daa*. If you speak French, then I suggest you talk to yourself in French for the rest of the night; try to dream in French if you can. That's how you'll know you're fluent in French. If not, then just mumble garbage to yourself in a French accent. Dream in that mumbled garbage as well. (That's how you know you're fluent in mumbled garbage.) Stare at yourself in the mirror while eating and put on a beret. Maybe pull out some Sartre or Simone De Beauvoir.

You have now carved out a whole beautiful night of borderline Parisian vacation for yourself without spending much of your hard-earned cash. If you post a pic, the next day at work, everyone will be like, "Hey, did you fly to Europe last night? That was so fast."

Please feel free to ignore this plan, even though it's an amazing one. It is not a part of the recipe. It's simply an example of all the ways chicken can change your life. Other character suggestions I have are a sixty-year-old woman at her house in the Hamptons in a Nancy Meyers movie, or a cool *Homo erectus* in her cave, enjoying all the marrow from the last bit of bones before her cave-mate comes home and takes it all. I suppose you can also just be yourself eating something delicious at home, having not spent a lot of money at all. Perhaps this is the best option, but who's to say?

---

* I have benefited from working at places where you can steal bottles of wine without anyone noticing. When you are young, loot alcohol whenever possible. I don't mean from stores, but just, like, if someone takes you to their house and you're not into it, but they seem rich, one hundo percent "borrow" some booze. Or if you don't finish a bottle of wine at a restaurant, put that shit under your shirt and take it with you. (Best if you're already drunk when doing this. Stealing is easier while drunk.)

I think it's fun to be reminded how far food can take you in one evening if you're just alone at home and broke. Forget your money problems for a moment and fly away. You don't actually have to read Sartre. You can just watch *When Harry Met Sally*. Clearly that's what I do, but I leave a copy of Sartre next to me, just in case some hot philosopher happens to be walking around my apartment.

Au revoir, mes petits poulets.

P.S. This recipe suggests a cast iron skillet. Did you not get one yet? Are you literally insane? It's life changing! Go right now and buy one.

kk. Love you.

CHEAP CHICKEN LEGS

INGREDIENTS

2 tablespoons extra-virgin olive oil, plus more for the skillet

2 medium sweet potatoes, scrubbed and cut into 1-inch cubes (leave the peel on)

½ medium onion, cut into 1-inch pieces

6–8 cloves garlic, peeled

2 whole chicken legs, skin on

1 teaspoon salt

1 teaspoon pepper

½ bunch kale, destemmed and chopped roughly

Chopped parsley, for garnish

DIRECTIONS

• Preheat the oven to 475°F.

• Lightly coat a 12-inch cast iron skillet (or another heavy-bottomed, ovenproof frying pan) with olive oil.

• In a mixing bowl, combine the sweet potatoes, onion, and garlic cloves. Drizzle with 2 tablespoons of olive oil and mix well to coat.

• Place the chicken legs skin-side up in the oiled pan.

• Arrange the vegetable mixture around the chicken, making sure the chicken is mostly exposed.

• Sprinkle the chicken and vegetables with the salt and pepper.

• Bake for 35 minutes.

• Add the chopped kale to the pan, stirring gently to ensure it is lightly coated with the oil pooling in the pan.

• Return to the oven for another 12 to 15 minutes, until the kale is wilted and the chicken skin is crisp.

• Let rest for 2 to 3 minutes, then serve hot, garnished with the parsley.

SERVES 2

BEGGAR'S PURSES, OR HOW TO TRICK YOUR PARENTS INTO PAYING YOUR RENT

MPB

Listen, there comes a point when no matter how proud you are, you just need help. Not everyone has the option of tricking their parents[*] into paying their rent, but if you're lucky enough to have it, then please follow the directions below. We are firm believers that most problems can be solved with a little bit of manipulation. We don't want you to have to come out and ask your parents, or sugar daddy, or rich uncle, to help you out. We want to do the classic thing of making them think it was their idea.

First: Make sure your appearance shows just how hard you are struggling. Get some purple makeup and draw bags under your eyes so they know just how difficult your life is. Quite possibly you won't have to do this because you will actually be that exhausted! It's also important to poke holes into your clothes. Again, this may not be necessary because you probably already own a pair of ripped jeans or a shirt with holes in it because they are cool. When some Old makes the following remark: "Did you buy those jeans like that?" say, "No, actually. It's just because I wear them so much." They'll be taken aback. Serves them right.

Next: Make sure your apartment is absolutely spotless, save for your bills. Leave them in a pile. When they are noticed, just say: "Oops, I was just going over those." Your parents will realize how responsible you are. I know you get e-bills, but print them out. Also, write up fake invoices and add those to the pile. Examples: *$200 for homonymic device pad for living a wholesome life*, or *$7,003 for capademic polioside to stop pesticide*. These are not real things, but if your parents ask what they are, just be like, "They are millennial tools for survival." Your parents will feel old and drop the subject.

Scatter your apartment with self-help articles you've printed from the internet. You obviously cannot afford books (apart from this one). Also, and this is important, make a trophy case for any accolades you've won over the years, so your parents are reminded how proud of you they are. If you got a nice email from your boss, print it out. Put it next to the basketball

---

[*] Please note that this recipe can be used not only on your parents, but also on other people you'd like to manipulate. For example, invite your landlord over for dinner. Let her see just how in need of help you are, and how much you are trying. She won't cover your rent, but maybe she'll let you slide for a few weeks, or forever, or maybe she'll fall in love with you. Who's to say? Anything is possible.

trophy you got for "best effort" in eighth grade. Remind your parents that you are and have always been a true success, especially in their eyes.

Optional: Promise a drink to anyone scary looking but normal seeming who you see on the street. Tell a bunch of them to squat in your apartment silently during dinner so your parents think you have eight to ten roommates. (You may also ask friends of yours, but random characters will rouse much more worry out of your creators.)

Finally: Arrange for a friend to call you several times throughout the night. Tell your parents it's "the debt collector." This friend can also arrive at your house and knock on the door wearing an old-timey hat. (It cannot be one of the same friends you are using as a fake squatting roommate. This will blow your gambit!)

Now, let's move on to the food. Beggar's purses are perfect for this meal; not only are they inexpensive to make, but they really shine a light on your problem, and are not subtle at all.

Gather the pouches together to look like hobo's purses. If you don't fold them correctly, this is the perfect time for a comment like "Jeez, I just can't do anything right." While the lentils will be delicious, they also allow for a second comment, like "Sorry, this is all I could afford. Did I mention how much I love you?"

Also, buy the cheapest wine you can and turn the bottle so the label faces them. Start crying at dinner. If you're nostalgic, the tears will probably come naturally; you won't have to act. At this point your parents should offer to help you out if they can. If they don't make the offer, cry harder and tell them what's wrong. This should seal the deal. *Cha-ching.*

All kidding aside, we love our parents, and we don't want to have to take their money. They've worked for it and it's their time to chill, but we need a little cushion, and if they can help us, so be it. If your parents can't help you financially, then hopefully they can help you in other ways, like with love, or really terrible advice. And if you can invite them over for dinner, then just do it: to say thank you, 'cause they raised you or whatever.

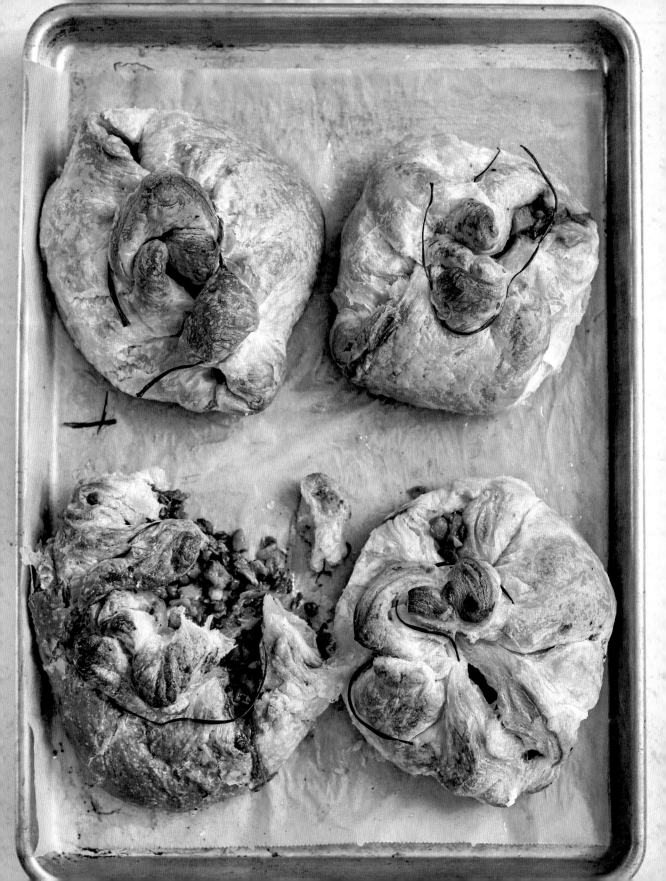

BEGGAR'S PURSES

INGREDIENTS

For the filling

4 tablespoons extra-virgin olive oil

2 medium onions, chopped

2 carrots, peeled and chopped

¼ pound white mushrooms, chopped

2 cloves garlic, finely chopped

1 (15-ounce) can cooked lentils, drained and rinsed

½ teaspoon salt

½ teaspoon pepper

½ cup cheap white wine

For the beggar's purses

4 sheets 4 × 4-inch puff pastry (you may have to trim the pastry to the exact size)

Extra-virgin olive oil, as needed

1 large handful fresh parsley, finely chopped, divided

1 tablespoon dried thyme, divided

4 chives or green onions

Salt and pepper

DIRECTIONS

Make the filling

- Place the oil in a large frying pan over medium heat.

- Add the onions, carrots, mushrooms, garlic, and lentils and let cook, stirring often, until vegetables are soft but not browned, about 15 minutes.

- Add the salt and pepper.

- Add the wine and cook until the liquid is almost entirely absorbed.

- Remove from heat and allow to cool.

Assemble the beggar's purses

- Preheat the oven to 375°F.

- Line a baking tray with parchment paper or brush it with olive oil.

- Place one sheet of puff pastry on your work surface.

- Brush a little oil all over the sheet and sprinkle one-quarter of the parsley and thyme over the top.

- In the middle of sheet, place one-quarter of the cooled filling, about ¾ cup.

- Pull all the sides up toward the center and pinch together at the top to make a purse.

- Tie the top of the purse with a chive or green onion by making a knot around the base of the crease.

- Brush the outside of each purse with oil and sprinkle with salt and pepper. Repeat the same procedure to make a total of four purses.

- Place the purses on the prepared baking tray.

- Bake for 17 to 20 minutes, or until the puff pastry purses become a light golden brown.

- Serve immediately.

SERVES 4

NO-CASH CAR CRASH CARBONARA

MPB

Hey, bad drivers. Let's chat, because you are in literally the best company.

So, let's say you bounced your rent check, but then somehow, through a mixture of looting, "borrowing" money from "friends," and cooking sensible meals from this book, you've made it through the week. Congratulations. You think you're home free, but something else comes up. Everyone has a little money-draining habit that they just can't kick, even when they're really broke. My fabulous habit is getting into very minor car accidents. This is how I learned not to kick that habit, but to deal with it and continue to eat well. Let me now weave you a tale.

I arrived in Los Angeles and after two weeks of "Confidence Driving" lessons from a man named Pablo, I decided to get a rental car and show off my new moves. On my first outing with the car, I left the lights on and burned out the battery. I had to call Andrew from the rental car company to jump-start it. On my second outing, I locked myself out of it during a hike in Runyon Canyon. (That's a canyon name drop, you guys. It's where Lauren used to hike on *The Hills*.) People would go up and come back down and see me still standing there, waiting, cell phone locked in my front seat. Again, had to call Andrew (from a stranger's phone). Finally, my third outing came and I promised myself this was the day I would make it work. Andrew would not get a call OR A TEXT today. I was running late to a meeting and driving around in circles looking for a parking spot, getting more and more anxious, when finally I hit someone. (I mean I hit another car, not a person; this isn't where I admit to manslaughter or a hit-and-run. I'm saving that for the next book.) Out of the car I hit emerged a teenage girl in the middle of her road test, along with her DMV supervisor. I approached them and immediately began profusely apologizing. The police came and the DMV instructor said I'd admitted culpability. I didn't think I had done anything of the sort. My natural state is just to apologize. I'm a girl; that's apparently what we do. I fought back, but the die had been cast. To this day, I am not sure who's to blame for that accident: Katarina, the sixteen-year-old, or myself. I do hope she got her license, though.

Once the crime scene was clear, I had to deal with the damage to my rental car, which was quite a lot. I called Andy-poo for the last time. He arrived and reminded me that I had not purchased insurance with the rental car and that I did not have any of my own. I had let him down. He towed the car, put me on the Do Not Rent list, and drove away with a disappointed look on his face. A week after getting my first car, I began paying off the damage to my first car. I also lost Andrew as a friend.

For my second car, I went to Rent-A-Wreck, a glorious place where I feel completely at home. It's okay if you dent the cars from Rent-A-Wreck! They're already pieces of shit! I took home a beautifully dinged-up bright blue Kia SUV with no air-conditioning, and quite shortly after doing so, I backed it into the Prius of a *very* prominent Los Angeles jeweler. A kind man, he didn't take my insurance (which I now had). Instead he called me once a week to make sure I was working to pay him back. I would shake with fear listening to his voicemails. I couldn't bear to ever pick up his calls. Finally, I got my $800 together. I walked into his diamond shop with my little check and our exchange was done. Now I'm on his Christmas card list. One day I will wear his jewels to the Oscars and I will remind him of this, and then he will take them away from me and I will be jewelry-naked at the Oscars.

After these two accidents, I really started to get down on myself. I felt like an idiot. I was making no money, looking for a steady job, and the second I got it I would have to start paying off two accidents, plus a bunch of minor scrapes that aren't as fun to recount. I really thought I should move home and live at the foot of my parents' bed like a groundhog forever. And just as I was finalizing my plans to do this, I got a job. So I would have to get yet another car, a non-rented car, a car that would truly be mine.

I got a used silver Nissan Altima with no radio, best suited for a family of five. I planned to do my best not to damage this car, but that was obviously not a plan I could follow. A week after getting the car, I was parking next to a bright red Mercedes convertible in a garage. Afraid of hitting the Mercedes, I parked my car extra close to the wall on the opposite side. I ended up scraping the entire left side of my car. The next week (and I'm not kidding about how quickly these accidents happened one after the other) I scraped the right side of the car when I ran into the entrance gate at Universal Studios Hollywood. All my coworkers came out to laugh at me and I held up tons of important Hollywood people that morning, but at least I made the scrapes on my car symmetrical, and symmetry is beauty.

Soon, I was getting into minor accidents all over town! I crashed my bumper into my own garage. I backed into a teen celebrity in Silver Lake. I backed into two Australian tourists. I backed into a Spanish man and his blind wife on Yom Kippur, the day in the Jewish religion when you purge yourself of all sins. I got flat tires on highways galore and knocked off both my side mirrors.

My car had gone from lightly used to something you could get at Rent-A-Wreck in a matter of weeks, and I felt really terrible about it, but I also learned some things. Obviously, I needed to be a more careful driver, but that wasn't going to happen overnight. That was going to take time. (That is still taking time.) But I also learned that I couldn't torture myself every

time I hit my car against something. As long as everyone involved in my accident was safe—and so far, they have been—there was no reason to hate myself over it. I couldn't go home and pout. I had to go on living my life. Running over a brick and getting a flat tire doesn't mean you sit on the highway crying and cancel your date, it means you call AAA, sit in your car crying, and then go to your date a little late with your mascara running. I thought of this really smart phrase, *shit happens*, and well, it does and you've got to move on.

How this relates to food is as follows: You may be poor right now, and the second a new bill comes up, like one from a car accident, you may think, "Okay, Gabi and Miranda are wrong. I can't eat well. I'm even broker than I was before!" But that's just not true. We promise these meals will help you at your absolute brokest. More important, you will need them the most at your absolute brokest, because that is when you may feel the shittiest. After you crash your car, or your equivalent of crashing your car, you need something like carbonara to remind you that you're okay. Don't panic to pay your bills overnight. Set up a payment plan that allows you to live your daily life as best you can.

And if your problem, like mine, is expensive minor car accidents, then let me leave you with a final thought: Never get anything (cosmetic) fixed. If your car is safe to drive but looks like shit, who cares? Scratches are charming and create a cool damsel-in-distress vibe. Plus people will always give you the best parking spots because they're afraid of you and want you off the road. Save your money for food, and clothes, and fun.

Anyhow, enjoy the carbonara.

Love,

A really great driver

NO-CASH CAR CRASH CARBONARA

INGREDIENTS

8 ounces dried spaghetti

2 strips uncooked bacon

3 cloves garlic, sliced

2 eggs, lightly beaten

½ cup grated Parmesan

Salt and pepper

DIRECTIONS

- Cook the spaghetti according to package directions in salted boiling water. Drain, reserving ¼ cup of the cooking water.

- Heat a large dry frying pan over medium-high heat. Cook the bacon strips for 2 to 3 minutes on each side, or until brown and crisp. Discard all but 1 tablespoon of the bacon fat. Dry the bacon on paper towels and let cool. When it is cool enough, chop or crumble the bacon and set aside.

- Cook the sliced garlic in the reserved bacon fat over medium heat for 30 seconds, or just until fragrant.

- Add the drained pasta and the reserved cooking water and toss together using tongs. Cook for 1 minute, or until cooking liquid begins to absorb.

- Remove the pan from heat, add the eggs, and mix thoroughly. Continue tossing the pasta with one hand, to avoid scrambling the eggs, and add the Parmesan. Toss well. Add the crumbled bacon, season with salt and pepper to taste (careful with the salt—the bacon is already salty), and serve hot.

SERVES 2

TRYING TO MAKE ENDS MEET TOFU

MPB

You know the feeling. It's that night of the week when you get home super late from work. It's probably a Wednesday, but it feels like a Thursday and you're super bummed when you realize it's not. Meanwhile, you didn't have any time to stop at the supermarket and you're starving. You're broke and have almost nothing in the refrigerator. Dinner means taking very drastic measures. Dumpster diving? Eating your exfoliating creams? Stealing?

Do you steal food from your friends and family? I did.

It started young, probably around age six or seven. Late at night, I would be bored and afraid of going to bed. Tossing and turning, I'd decide to quickly run to the kitchen and open the refrigerator door. In the bottom-right drawer there was a secret bag of mini Hershey's bars. I'd grab a few and jet. If my parents heard a rustle, they'd say, "What's that?" and I'd sprint away screaming, "Noooooothing!" Then I'd get back into bed and put the chocolates under my knees until they were warm enough to eat. I slept satisfied, but then I wanted more (of both chocolate and stealing).

I had my next chance at thievery when I went to an all-girls' sleepaway camp for the summer. At camp, each girl in my bunk was sent a giant trunk of candy by her parents. I don't know why this happened; perhaps all the parents were afraid their daughters would have lame personalities without sugar highs. My parents had more confidence in me, so I didn't get any candy. Instead, I got one small bag of Doritos and a training sports bra. I finished the Doritos as soon as I got them, so I had no choice but to steal. I'd wait for a time when all the other girls were out of the bunk and take a little piece of candy from each one. I had an accomplice for a bit, but she realized my behavior was too risky and bailed. I continued on my own. I did it every day until I had a nice moderate stash of my own. And then I was happy, but my stealing bug did not go away.

It only got worse in college. I basically had no business being in a sorority, which meant I was often home while the other girls were out. I stole pounds and pounds of frozen yogurt from our minifridge. People would yell and scream. They would write threatening emails about missing yogurt: "Honestly, fuck whoever took my yogurt. That's really uncool and immature, you guys. You're my sisters, but I literally hate you." Stuff like that. (I certainly wasn't the only culprit, just the best.)

There were also constant complaints of missing hummus and tofu. I'd never cop to it, but it was me. I ate your mashed-up chickpeas and frozen tofu! Not all of it, though! I used my camp tactics and took a little bit from everyone. And anyhow, I think all of your reactions to

the missing tofu were a little over-the-top. Tofu is like tampons. It's free for girls, and you're not a feminist if you don't share.

Now I am a sort-of adult, and when I get home from work exhausted at 10 p.m., I long to go back to my old ways. I want to sneak into my next-door neighbor Sammy's apartment and take an apple or a few veggie chips, or just take a whole pint of her garbage-tasting fake ice cream. I have her keys and I have done it before, but I need to change. I need to kick the habit.

Getting home late from work is the easiest time to forgo eating well and just cry yourself to sleep, eating nothing or eating garbage. Maybe you feel like you don't deserve a good dinner because you can't afford it. I obviously felt like I was being denied something back in my criminal days. But I deserve a good dinner now, even late at night when I feel shitty. I need not atone for my stealing sins by going hungry. So instead of stealing, I take a page out of the book of the girls I stole from and eat what they would eat. I always keep an extra package of tofu in my fridge for desperate nights like this because now I deserve my own.

This is dedicated to you, ladies who I stole from. My gift to you is this recipe. Eat it at 10 p.m. when you get home from work, when you're feeling bad like I did in college. I'm sorry I stole, but frankly, I'd do it again, and I think you all liked having something to get riled up about.

TRYING TO MAKE ENDS MEET TOFU

INGREDIENTS

1 (16-ounce) package extra-firm tofu, preferably sprouted

2 tablespoons coconut, vegetable, canola, or grapeseed oil

A few pinches salt

3 tablespoons store-bought teriyaki sauce

2 green onions, chopped

DIRECTIONS

- Wrap the tofu block in a clean dish towel and gently pat it dry. Cut the tofu into 1½-inch pieces (we like triangles).

- Heat the oil in a large frying pan over medium-high heat.

- Add the tofu to the pan, salt it well, and let cook, undisturbed, for 4 to 5 minutes (check after 4 to be sure it's not burning), until a thick golden-brown crust develops.

- Use a spatula or wooden spoon to flip the tofu as well as you can, to cook the other side until it is also golden brown and crispy.

- Add the teriyaki sauce and stir well to coat. Let cook for 2 to 3 minutes, until the sauce bubbles.

- Stir in the green onions.

- Remove from heat, transfer to a bowl, and serve immediately.

SERVES 2

CHAPTER 2

Cooking for Your Ever-Changing Moods

People say millennials are really narcissistic and too into themselves, but I don't know what they're talking about. I think we're all great. And I think everyone is really interested in our feelings, and mine in particular. Don't you agree?

On a recent trip home to visit my parents, I was complaining to them about how melancholy I felt. It was really getting in the way of my having a good time or enjoying myself at all. After about five to seven hours of charming whining, my dad had had enough. He got up from his desk chair, stopped his solitaire game (which he NEVER does) and said: "Stop paying so much goddamn attention to your moods! What's wrong with you? Get a life!" I recoiled! First of all, Dad, "Get a life?" Come on, be cool! And second of all, I'm a perfect person with too many feelings! Sorry that you're a repressed maniac!

Stop paying attention to my moods? Was he insane? Paying attention to my moods is my livelihood and also my absolute favorite thing to do. Is it a way to avoid moving forward or doing work? Certainly! But tracking my moods and keeping them in check is my number one priority. It comes before family, work, relationships, illness, and world peace! Anything at all!

For example, here is a day in my life:

6:30 a.m.: Wake up to pit in my stomach so deep and filled with so much neurosis that I know I simply cannot make it through the day. Also, sort of tired.

8:00 a.m.: See old man in my building put on a newsboy cap and go out for a walk. Feel the weight of both his and my own mortality on my shoulders. I am basically Atlas with the globe on my back.

10:00 a.m.: Receive a DM from an internet crush. Manically happy. Smiling so large I think it will erase every future wrinkle I've spent my whole life frowning onto my face.

11:30 a.m.: Get a compliment at work and feel good about it. Then immediately overstep boundaries and say something out of turn. Worry I have changed everyone's opinions of me forever. I'm a fraud. I don't belong in this career and everyone knows it. Eat approximately 18 peanut butter M&M's.

1:00 p.m.: Having not spoken a word since the 11:30 a.m. incident, I'm no longer sure who I am or what I'm doing on this planet. Am depleted. I open my notes app on my phone and journal feverishly.

2:00 p.m.: There is hope. Crush DM'ed me again! Only, he wants the email address of the other girl in my profile photo. Sink deeper into despair. I am unlovable and defective.

2:30 p.m.: Am in my head and miss something at work. Someone else does a better job than I do. Rage, jealousy, eat 118 peanut butter M&M's.

2:31 p.m.: I calm down. Everything will be fine.

2:32 p.m.: Realize thought at 2:31 p.m. was insane and resume feeling of impending doom.

2:33–5:59 p.m.: Period of numbness. Emotions are hard. Must dissociate.

6:00 p.m.: See dermatologist. She's not at all thrilled about the improvements in my skin. It's as though none of my accomplishments matter to anyone and I will never do anything of importance.

7:00 p.m.: Call mother on drive home. She asks if I'm in love or "happy." I hang up on her and an overwhelming sense of nostalgia washes over me.

7:30 p.m.: Get home. Night is shot. My moods were too intense today. I can't do any work or socialize now. I owe it to myself to eat 4,000 peanut butter M&M's.

See what I mean? Wasn't that cool? Wasn't driving myself mad just, like, a really killer use of time?

If I'm going to pay that much attention to my moods, shouldn't I also be eating specifically for them? And devoting even more time to figuring out exactly what emotion I'm experiencing at every moment and what food would pair with it too? Like food with wine. Eating for moods.

We've done the work for you! Please enjoy while you're crying. —MPB

I WANT TO PUNCH YOU IN THE FACE PASTA

GLM

You know how sometimes in movies a man will say to a woman, "You're so beautiful/hot/sexy when you're angry"? Well, I can say with great certainty that I was not the inspiration for that line.

First of all, I rarely exhibit outward signs of anger. (Now, inward . . .) Second, on the rare occasion that I do, I'm pretty sure it's not hot, as anger usually makes me nervous, inarticulate, and even a bit teary . . . leading me to my third point, which is that I generally avoid confrontation like the plague, and nobody ever looked sexy while desperately trying to change the subject.

When I discovered that a dude I thought was dating only me was, in fact, not, it felt like I'd been sucker-punched. I was hurt and sad, but mostly I was furious. As the weeks passed, my anger only got worse. How could he have done that to me? How could I have been so stupid? Would this feeling ever go away? He had little to say for himself when I confronted him. "Look, these things happen," he mumbled from his work line, which I called after he ignored my texts and calls to his cell for an entire week. "It's not like we were married or anything." I felt discarded, like a forgotten-about tampon you suddenly realize you should have removed hours ago. He was toxic and I was shocked.

My anger was very much alive . . . and I had no idea what to do with it. My cheeks felt hot and my heart pounded at first. I found myself spitting out complete sentences—great sentences—and cracking truly funny, if bitter, jokes. I was angry and vengeful, but also felt kind of sexy, like Detective Olivia Benson on the trail of a serial killer. I didn't recognize this cutting, sharpened version of myself, but I didn't dislike her.

This went on for weeks. I fell asleep mad; I woke up mad. My appetite was diminished, but it didn't bother me—I secretly relished exploring this new emotion. I felt powerful and in control for once. Every moment I spent hate-stalking his Facebook page made my fury increase, but I was addicted. I was a rage goddess and I wasn't sorry about it.

In the midst of my rage-goddess fury, I went out for Italian food with my friend Nada. I scanned the menu, unable to imagine eating, practically hissing at the busboys. But eventually my eyes landed on Spaghetti all'Arrabbiata. According to the menu, "Arrabbiata" comes from the Italian word "arrabbiato," which means "angry," a nod to this sauce's fiery heat. Perfect.

The tomato-based pasta was peppery and hot, thanks to the large amount of red chili flakes added to it. For the first time in recent memory, my appetite returned. The spicy sauce made

my eyes water, but it wasn't because I was upset. I left dinner that night feeling better for the first time in a long time—and also eager to perfect arrabbiata sauce at home.

The secret to the sauce is simple: crushed chilies. They get toasted in extra-virgin olive oil, which releases their own oils, creating a hot and deeply flavorful sauce that also features garlic, onions, and tomatoes. I add cool, creamy goat cheese to the top, which works like yogurt sauce (raita) alongside a hot Indian curry, cooling the palate with each spicy bite.

Rage spirals are a part of life, especially when idiot man-children don't take responsibility for their terrible actions. But spicy pasta with creamy goat cheese really can help.

I WANT TO PUNCH YOU IN THE FACE PASTA

INGREDIENTS

6 tablespoons extra-virgin olive oil

1 tablespoon red chili flakes (more or less to taste)

3 cloves garlic, finely chopped

½ medium yellow onion, finely chopped

1 (15-ounce) can diced tomatoes, with their juice

8 ounces long-strand pasta, like spaghetti or fettuccine

Salt and pepper

4 ounces crumbled goat cheese

DIRECTIONS

• Heat the oil in a large, heavy-bottomed frying pan or pot over medium heat.

• Add the chili flakes and cook for 2 to 3 minutes, stirring occasionally.

• Add the garlic and onion and cook for another 4 to 5 minutes, until soft.

• Add the tomatoes, stir well, and cover.

• Reduce heat to medium-low and cook, covered, for 18 to 22 minutes, stirring once or twice.

• Meanwhile, cook the pasta in salted boiling water according to package directions and drain.

• Taste the sauce and season with salt and pepper to taste.

• Toss the pasta with the sauce until each strand is well coated. Season with more salt and pepper if needed.

• Serve the pasta hot, on plates or in bowls, topped with a scattering of the goat cheese.

SERVES 2

MY BOSS IS A BITCH BANANA BREAD

GLM & MPB

Hey guys, here's a secret that you may not know. Miranda sure as hell didn't know it until Gabi taught her, but banana bread is really fucking easy to make. It's, like, the easiest thing on earth.

That is why it is the best thing to use to get back at your boss for being a total asshole or cunt. (Are we allowed to use the word *cunt*? We would never say it out loud, but it's easier to bear in writing and it makes us feel empowered and edgy, like we're young twin Patti Smiths.) (No, we hate it. Never use it.)

So you get home in a rage after being told your T-shirt is transparent and shows your bra. "Umm, that's not my fault," you say. "That's Alexander Wang's fault and the trickle-down economics of fashionable see-through T-shirts." Your anger is righteous. Now put that rage to use and make banana bread to get back at your boss. You have a few options for how to do so.

OPTION 1: Get rid of your boss in one fell swoop. Make banana bread for the entire office, but poison one special loaf for your boss. This is perhaps the riskiest plan, and you might end up going to jail for it, but at least you'll stop getting 4 a.m. phone calls (or if you do, they'll only be from your attorney). You can probably be creative, though. Send the banana bread as part of a gift basket supposedly from a client. Frame someone? We don't know. We leave that stuff up to you. Watch *The Talented Mr. Ripley* and get some ideas. You'll also have to figure out how to get the poison on your own. We hear arsenic is the most popular, but despite Miranda's constant begging, Gabi refused to write a recipe for poison. (If you have a good one, please find a way to contact Miranda. She swears she won't use it. She just thinks it's cool to know how to make poison.)

OPTION 2: More of a long con, but less likely to end with your incarceration. As previously stated, banana bread is very easy to make. This means you can make it every night, or in bulk. Bring it in to work every morning for breakfast. The office folk will get used to it and start to love you for it. Not to mention, your office crush will begin to see you in a new baking light. Your boss might even be jealous of all your new work friends and the camaraderie. (Lack of work friends may be the source of their anger. Everyone has something. Maybe you'll get lucky and hit a nerve.)

Now, let us get to the meat of the plan: Always bring in a special personal loaf for your calorie-counting, weight-obsessed boss. This works only if yours is the kind of boss whose entire personality is based on order and sliced turkey. Hopefully the boss will eat the banana bread every morning. It will just be sitting there taunting them and they will gain weight. If the weight isn't coming on

continue to ea...
You're great. Thanks!

fast enough, or if the loaf isn't being finished every day (which will be hard, because it will be so tasty), you can take further measures. Instead of getting all *Mr. Ripley*, get all *Mean Girls*. Don't add poison, but remember Kälteen bars? Lindsay Lohan gave them to Rachel McAdams in a ploy to get rid of her "hot bod," and therefore her power. Take a page from Lohan's book and add some weight-gain powder to your banana bread. You can get it at your local body-building supply store. Before you know it, this control freak boss of yours will be confused and scared. They will be stripped of the armor that came only from their tight bod. They'll have no choice but to be nicer, as it will seem their empire has fallen. Either that, or they'll just be kind of annoyed for a few weeks! You may feel guilty about causing this weight gain. Don't! At least you didn't commit murder.

OPTION 3: After fattening your boss up, cook her in a stew. (Again, there is no recipe for this because Gabi is "against cooking people." And also, this makes you a cannibal, but at least, like, a fun young one!) It should be fun.

OPTION 4: Get caught. Get fired. Or just be bad at your job and get fired. Collect severance package. Figure out what's next. Examine your life, etc.

OPTION 5: Quit, after an amazing speech. Not *Ripley*, not *Mean Girls*, but *Jerry Maguire*. Go home and get unemployment. Banana bread is cheap and you can subsist on it for a while.

OPTION 6: Stick it out, and make yourself a treat when you get home. (This is the lamest option, in our opinions.)

MY BOSS IS A BITCH BANANA BREAD

INGREDIENTS

2–3 very ripe bananas, peeled

⅓ cup melted butter or coconut, canola, or other vegetable oil

1 teaspoon baking soda

Pinch of salt

⅔ cup brown sugar

1 egg, lightly beaten

1 teaspoon vanilla extract

1½ cups all-purpose flour

½ cup dark or semisweet chocolate chips (optional)

⅓ cup toasted pecans or walnuts (optional)

DIRECTIONS

- Preheat the oven to 350°F and grease a 4 × 8-inch loaf pan.

- In a mixing bowl, mash the bananas with a fork until smooth.

- Stir the melted butter or oil into the mashed bananas.

- Mix in the baking soda and salt. Stir in the brown sugar, egg, and vanilla extract.

- Stir in the flour.

- Stir in the chocolate chips and nuts, if using.

- Pour the batter into your prepared loaf pan.

- Bake for 50 to 55 minutes, or until a toothpick inserted into the center comes out clean.

- Remove from oven and let cool completely.

- Remove the banana bread from the pan. Slice and serve.

SERVES 6 TO 8

REGRET RISOTTO

MPB

To my very bitter, self-doubting, second-guessing best friends,

I love you and feel your pain.

Boy oh boy, do I love a good regret. You know those people who say, "Life's too short, you can't regret things"? Well, I think they're dumb. Regrets are amazing. Holding on to them is super fun and keeps you sane. For example:

I regret that I was a C-section baby and couldn't come out the normal way. I know I didn't have much control, but I feel it fucked me up.

I regret going to a big state school and joining a sorority. It was the wrong place for me, and I couldn't thrive there or become the person I was meant to be. I hold on tightly to this regret so it can hold me back and remind me now that I am not currently the best version of myself.

I regret that at that college, I didn't kiss my male best friend the night he asked me to go home with him. I regret that I didn't experience what that relationship could have been and what I would have learned from it because I was afraid of it. I hold on to this regret because it reminds me that I am probably stunted in current relationships because of what I missed out in that one, which should have been my first real relationship.

I regret that while abroad in Dublin, I didn't kiss my female best friend on our last night. She was the coolest bisexual girl I'd ever met/seen. (She taught me it was sometimes hot to show off your cellulite through white jeans.) She kissed me on the cheek and said, "You're precious." I should have gone for the whole thing.

I regret not buying this one orange taffeta dress I saw on sale in 2008. I wear a lot of black and I feel this probably could have helped my wardrobe and life in a HUGE way.

I regret washing my face with exfoliating-bead cleanser from the years 2011 to 2014 because I think a lot of those beads have built up in my eyes over time and I'm probably going totally blind.

I regret never dating a motorcycle dude. I'm not sure where I'd find one, but I'd like to live out my *Grease 2* fantasy. Gabi did and it seems fun.

I regret not writing a senior thesis. It would have won a Pulitzer. I know it.

I regret not going to graduate school, where I would have won my second Pulitzer.

I regret not taking the MCAT. (Kidding.)

I regret every time I've gotten too drunk (except for three times, which were actually very productive).

I regret not keeping up a relationship with my college creative writing professor. He was the first person who truly believed in me and I was frightened by how different I was from him and how much he may have expected from me. If we'd remained close, I'd definitely be a better writer, or at least I'd be closer to being the kind of writer I'd one day like to be.

I regret that I'm always late. And that once I arrive late, I make the entire meal about apologizing for how late I was.

I regret this one time I slept till 5 p.m. and forgot to wish my mom a happy birthday.

I regret that I'm so afraid of things.

I regret that I regret all these things so hard.

And so I'm going to try to get rid of them in my Regret Risotto. I'm going to stir them all away and hopefully feel a little bit better about everything. I don't trust psychics. I don't do yoga. And I can't meditate; I've tried. But I can stir! (I think.)

Perhaps you're not like me, trying to rid yourself of every regret of your life.

Perhaps you only regret partying too hard last night, or buying a pair of shoes, or binge-watching something. Well, this risotto should lessen the pain of those things as well.

Think of it as just risotto, or think of it as a witchy potion to wash away all your pain. I think the latter is more fun. Wait, did I not mention that I'm an actual witch? I'm like a super angsty millennial witch with a Twitter feed. There's a YA novel about me coming out soon.

NOTE: While we can't guarantee the witchcraft effect of this dish, it is necessary to stir a lot when you make risotto, so you may as well suspend your disbelief, put on a witch's hat, and start memorizing spells. You can do this even if you have no regrets at all, but I feel like most witches have a lot of regrets. I feel like it's part of their deal. Get stirring.

REGRET RISOTTO

INGREDIENTS

2 tablespoons extra-virgin olive oil

2 shallots, finely chopped

1 cup uncooked Arborio rice

3½ cups vegetable or chicken stock (or water)

½ cup frozen green peas

Juice and zest of 1 lemon

⅛ cup grated Parmesan

½ teaspoon salt, plus more for seasoning

½ teaspoon pepper, plus more for seasoning

8 large shrimp, peeled and deveined (you can buy them this way)

1 tablespoon unsalted butter

3 tablespoons mascarpone cheese, plus more for garnish

DIRECTIONS

- Heat the olive oil in a large pot over medium heat. Add the shallots and cook for 1 to 2 minutes, or until soft and fragrant. Add the rice and allow to toast for 2 to 3 minutes, stirring occasionally to avoid scorching.

- Add the stock, ½ cup at a time, stirring throughout cooking to encourage absorption. Continue cooking and stirring until all the stock has been absorbed and the rice has become very creamy. This should take about 20 minutes.

- Stir in the peas, lemon juice, Parmesan, and ½ teaspoon each salt and pepper.

- Season the shrimp with a pinch each of salt and pepper.

- Melt the butter in a medium nonstick frying pan over medium-high heat.

- Add the shrimp and cook for 2 to 3 minutes per side, just until they turn pink and firm. Remove from heat.

- Gently stir the 3 tablespoons of mascarpone into the risotto.

- To serve, divide the risotto into bowls and top each bowl with a small spoonful of mascarpone, a pinch of the lemon zest, and a few shrimp.

SERVES 2 TO 3

MERCURY IS IN RETROGRADE MANGO SMOOTHIE

MPB

Perhaps not all of you are familiar with the idea of Mercury being in retrograde. Let me explain: Mercury is the planet situated closest to the sun. This means its orbit is much shorter than Earth's. About three or four times a year, Mercury speeds past Earth, appearing to move backward in its orbit, and we, as a unified human planet, experience the effects of Mercury being in retrograde.

Apparently Mercury is in control of communication and, like, clear thinking and truth and travel and painting and spin class and everything, so when Mercury goes backward, all those things do too. If you already have trouble thinking clearly, you go berserk. If you're a hot mess, you become basically a hot stinking load of garbage.

I didn't learn about Mercury being in retrograde until I moved to Los Angeles, and obviously I identified it as complete bullshit. I don't believe in astrology. I will roll my eyes at you if you bring it up at a dinner party. Does this make me unfeminine? Does this make me a skeptic? I can live with that. Because I think astrology is dumb. But I have since changed my mind on one specific thing. I am now a young woman who believes in the terrible effects of Mercury being in retrograde. And this is something I have to live with.

Do I mostly like having a new thing to blame all my problems on? Of course! There is no greater joy for me than crying in my car, listening to Belinda Carlisle, only to realize that Mercury is in retrograde and maybe I also have my period. That destructive behavior wasn't me! It was my hormones! And the planet! And everything my parents did to me growing up! I AM PERFECT. I DID NOTHING WRONG. I AM JUST IN RETROGRADE.

They say that when Mercury is in retrograde, you shouldn't start any new projects or relationships. They say you shouldn't even leave your house, but there's a difference between accepting astrology and being insane. I prefer to start at least sixteen new crafts projects, plan one exotic vacation, and enter into ten new romantic relationships all at once, but you can make your own decisions.

However you spend your retrograde, you can enjoy this mango smoothie. It's light and fresh and it can pull you out of the slump as much as the universe will allow. The blender does most of the work for you, since during retrograde, you are basically an invalid. Don't drink it near your computer, or a diamond tiara, or your passport. You will spill it. You *can* add a shot of vodka if retrograde is really killing ya. (I did not consult Gabi on this. I'm sure it's fine.)

Once Mercury is out of retrograde, you have to resume your normal patterns of behavior. You can no longer skip work to catch up on every episode ever of *RuPaul's Drag Race* and then claim the universe made you do it.

You can drink this smoothie whenever you want, though.

MERCURY IS IN RETROGRADE MANGO SMOOTHIE

INGREDIENTS

2 cups frozen cubed mango (or 2 fresh mangoes, peeled, pitted, and cubed)

1 cup yogurt (Greek or regular, any fat percentage; nondairy yogurt works, too)

1¼ cups milk (any fat percentage, or nondairy)

3–4 fresh mint leaves

DIRECTIONS

• Place all ingredients in a blender and blend for at least 30 seconds, or until smooth.

• If the smoothie is too thick, add a little more milk to thin it out.

• Divide between 2 glasses and serve immediately.

SERVES 2

MY EX IS ENGAGED ENCHILADAS

GLM

My ex didn't take very long to fall in love after we broke up. In fact, I'm pretty sure he was halfway to the altar with his now-wife when we were still dating. It was one of those relationships that, in retrospect, was so stupid to dive into (oh hey there, bitter divorce and substantial age difference!), but the inimitable trifecta of attraction, oxytocin, and unresolved authority issues drove me straight into his arms before I could reconsider.

When I learned he had gotten engaged to someone new just a few months after he had abruptly stopped returning my phone calls (I'd call it *ghosting* but this was, like, 2011 and such lingo didn't yet exist), I was hurt and angry. When I did the math and discovered he'd been seeing us both at the same time (thanks, Facebook photo time-stamping!), I was the most livid I'd been in my entire life, and it was unlike anything I'd ever experienced. My cheeks felt hot and my heart pounded. No chamomile tea or Xanax could soothe me; no call to my therapist or mom or best friend could ease my pain. I was a woman scorned.

For weeks, I lived in a bubble of my own fury, alternately crying and going for "hate runs," which were more stomping than they were jogging (but still great cardio!). Finally my best friend took pity on me and insisted I join her family at a cabin in Lake Tahoe for the weekend. I loaded up my car and set off on the long drive to the mountains by myself. "Alone again, as usual," I seethed.

The drive was rough. Lots of traffic, and heavy snow as I got higher and higher up. The universe was actually spitting in my face. Somewhere around Nevada City, my car needed gas and I needed to eat. I filled up the tank and pulled into a tiny Tex-Mex diner for a quick bite.

I ordered the vegetarian green chili enchiladas, sipped the weak, tepid coffee that had been poured for me before I had a chance to ask for it, and waited for what I expected would be a couple of corn tortillas filled with greasy cheese and oversalted sauce. *Whatever*, I thought. *It'll get me through the rest of the drive.*

When the waitress returned a few minutes later with my order, I was shocked and delighted by the plate in front of me: delicate corn tortillas folded around tender greens, perfectly seasoned potatoes, a very lightly spicy green chili sauce, and just enough cheese to bind everything together. I took a bite, closed my eyes, and savored the deliciousness. For the first time, my broken heart wasn't the only thing on my mind.

MY EX IS ENGAGED ENCHILADAS

INGREDIENTS

Extra-virgin olive oil

1 medium russet potato, scrubbed and diced

1 large or 2 medium sweet potatoes, scrubbed and diced

1 large bunch kale or Swiss chard, destemmed and thinly sliced

Salt and pepper

12 corn tortillas

2 (16-ounce) cans green enchilada sauce

2 cups shredded jack or cheddar cheese

DIRECTIONS

- Preheat the oven to 375°F.

- Grease a 9 x 13-inch baking dish with olive oil.

- Place the potatoes, sweet potatoes, and kale or chard in a large pot with enough water to cover over high heat. Cover with a fitted lid and bring to a boil.

- Once the water boils, reduce heat to medium-low and simmer until both kinds of potatoes are cooked through, about 10 minutes.

- Remove from heat, drain, season with salt and pepper to taste, and set aside.

- Microwave the tortillas for 30 seconds or so to soften them.

- Pour the enchilada sauce into a mixing bowl or baking dish.

- Dip a tortilla into the sauce and pull it out, shaking off excess sauce.

- Lay the tortilla on a flat surface. Place 2 to 3 tablespoons of potato-kale filling and a generous sprinkle of cheese in the center of the tortilla and roll it up.

- Place the rolled-up tortilla seam-side down in the prepared pan. Repeat with the remaining tortillas, sauce, filling, and cheese. Reserve about ½ cup cheese for the top.

- Pour the remaining sauce over all the rolled tortillas in the pan.

- Top with the reserved cheese.

- Bake for 30 to 35 minutes, or until the cheese is bubbly and browned.

- Serve hot.

SERVES 4 TO 6

QUARTER-LIFE CRISIS QUESO

GLM

My quarter-life crisis hit when I was twenty-seven. More specifically, it hit somewhere on I-10, on the way from Louisiana to Texas. I was driving with my best friend, Caitlin, who was moving from Nashville, where she had been living and practicing law for the past three years, to Sonoma, California, where she would be joining her father, also an attorney, at his practice.

As for what I'd been doing? Um . . . blogging? Working as an executive assistant? Going into debt?

I had no idea what I was doing with my life. Here was my beautiful, brilliant best friend—already an accomplished attorney, homeowner, and responsible caretaker of an adorable Boston terrier. I, on the other hand, couldn't seem to keep the succulent I inherited from one of my three roommates alive. It was hard not to compare myself to her.

When she asked me to make the two-week drive with her, I figured what the hell. It would be a great bonding experience for us, and a fourteen-day vacation from worrying about what the hell I was going to do with my life. (I worried a little bit about missing my weekly quidditch match, but I figured the team would be okay drinking butterbeer without me for a couple of weeks.)

We sampled a lot of Southern cuisine along our drive, the cheaper the better. When we reached Austin, Texas (a mecca of cheap, delicious food), we found queso and chips on nearly every menu. I have to admit, at first I was a little freaked out. I loved the idea of queso dip (essentially melted cheese), but it's typically made with uberprocessed cheese (think Velveeta), which gives it its plastic-like, easy meltability . . . and is, in my opinion, utterly disgusting. Seriously, it tastes like a melted-down Mattel factory. (Does that make me a snob? Probably a little. Sorry.)

At every restaurant we visited, I asked if the queso was made with processed cheese. If they told me yes, I refused to try it. I may have been clueless, but I was not unprincipled.

Finally we stopped at a little taco shack where the hostess informed me that their queso was made from real cheddar cheese, not the fake stuff. "We add a little evaporated milk and corn-starch to stabilize it, but other than that, it's all cheese and chilies." I was sold.

And of course, it was delicious. Spicy, creamy, and most important, authentic. If ever there was life guidance in the form of a cheese dip, this was it.

Try my take on their version on tortilla chips for ballpark-style nachos, drizzled over grilled beef and corn tortillas for Southwestified tacos, or even atop a bowl of hot chili. And the best part? It reheats like a dream.

QUARTER-LIFE CRISIS QUESO

INGREDIENTS

2 tablespoons butter

2 tablespoons cornstarch

1 (12-ounce) can evaporated milk

¼ cup cream cheese

8 ounces sharp cheddar cheese, shredded

1 (4-ounce) can chopped green chilies, or 1 fresh jalapeño, chopped

1 (15-ounce) can diced tomatoes, drained

½ teaspoon salt

Tortilla chips, for serving

DIRECTIONS

- Melt the butter in a medium saucepan over medium-high heat.

- Whisk in the cornstarch until combined and cook for 1 minute, stirring constantly.

- Add the evaporated milk and whisk until combined and smooth.

- Add the cream cheese and whisk until melted.

- Add half of the cheddar and stir until melted. Repeat with the rest of the cheddar.

- Stir in the green chilies and tomatoes until combined.

- Stir in the salt.

- Serve immediately with chips.

SERVES 4 TO 6

Before I turn 25:

- Find life purpose.
- Stop borrowing $ from Mom & Dad.
- Grad school?
- STOP DATING LOSERS.
- Cook every ~~night~~.
- ~~learn~~ to ~~date~~?
- ~~exercise~~ regularly.

I'M A FRAUD FRENCH TOAST

MPB

I live in fear. I know the police are coming to arrest me any day now. I'm not exactly sure what specific type of fraud I will be booked for, but by constantly spewing bullshit, all the time, always, I commit the act of fraud on a daily basis.

Maybe the officers can get me on identity theft? I didn't steal anyone's identity in particular, but I do know that the way I describe myself at cocktail parties has no relation to who I actually am. It's true, I have a master list of identities I'd like to steal hidden away in a safe (Jemima Kirke, Jenna Lyons, this cool-looking person I once saw on the street and now casually stalk), but there's no way the police force knows about that.

So why am I a fraud? Why do I deserve to spend tonight in a jail cell with murderous felons? Well, first of all, I call myself a comedy writer, but I'm not funny at all. The sixth-grade class wit, Will Harper, told me so in the back of the school bus in 2001 and I know it's true. So why in God's name am I writing this book? I mean; I'm not a writer. Sure, sometimes I tweet, but I definitely don't work as hard as I should. I should be locked away in a bunker like J. D. Salinger, writing my magnum opus. (My bunker would have a pilates studio or something in it. If I'm gonna bunker, I'm gonna bunker in style.) Further, everything good I have right now is the result of luck and not my own doing. I don't deserve my job or anything else. And I'm not even doing enough with the opportunities I do have. I could be doing so much more. (I know this twenty-one-year-old girl who's a Nobel laureate or some shit.) Someone else would be doing so much more with what I have. Also, and this is just a small thing, but I've lied about my weight on my driver's license, and everywhere else, since the beginning of time.

Shit, I hear a siren. The police are probably on their way right now. I wonder what kind of officers they send in situations like this. Are they, like, cool emotional police? Are their handcuffs made of mink because they know I'm not really a threat to anyone other than myself and the people I lie to on dates? I should start preparing. *Hmm.* I get one phone call, right? Should I call my mom? She'll definitely say I'm not a fraud, and I think a bunch of my friends and Snapchat followers believe in me too. Trouble is, I think I'll have to defend myself in this instance because I am the one imagining this metaphorical arrest. I can't defend myself! I'm full of shit and I know it. Send me to jail forever!

I don't want to go to jail yet though. I need to get through this season of Big Brother; I'm in a Draft! I'll have to get myself out of this. I guess I can believe in myself a little bit, at least, in front of the police, to trick them. Or I can lie about believing in myself? Can I pretend I'm confident? But how does one do this? Should I genuinely accept a compliment—the hardest task on earth?

New plan: I'll make them French toast when they arrive. My French toast is good, and when they tell me it's good, I'll believe them. They'll see that I can accept compliments without collapsing and let me go free. This is a perfect plan. Let me get cooking.

. . .

Okay, guys, I have finished the French toast. I am just going to take one bite to taste it. Wait, this is really good. This isn't even a trick. The French toast is actually great. Maybe I'm not a fraud. I made this breakfast all on my own. I'm semicompetent. Okay, maybe writing and being an adult aren't as easy as making French toast, but perhaps I can just acknowledge that I'm trying? Maybe everything good that has happened to me is because of me? Maybe it's not all luck? Maybe it's not the next great American novel I'm writing, but I am doing something, I think. Something is good, right? Things don't have to be impossible for them to be good. Wait, guys, I'm not a fraud. This is huge. This means the police aren't coming, which is important, because I finished all the French toast. At last I can relax. I'm gonna turn on the TV and finish my whole DVR tonight. No, actually I'm going to work.

Wait, shit, someone just buzzed my apartment. The police are here! And it's the real police. This might be about all those diamonds I stole earlier. I forgot to mention that movie, *Entrapment*, was based on me. Gotta go. Write me in prison!

I'M A FRAUD FRENCH TOAST

INGREDIENTS

2 eggs, lightly beaten

1 pint milk (any fat percentage will work, as will nondairy milk)

3 tablespoons granulated sugar

Zest of 1 lemon

12 (½-inch) slices of baguette or 6 slices of sourdough bread

2–3 tablespoons unsalted butter, for frying

¼ cup lemon curd or lemon marmalade

Powdered sugar, for serving (optional)

DIRECTIONS

- In a large mixing bowl, whisk together the eggs, milk, granulated sugar, and lemon zest.

- Dip each slice of bread into the egg-milk mixture, soaking both sides completely. Let soak for at least 2 minutes.

- Melt the butter in a large frying pan over medium-high heat.

- Cook the soaked bread slices, working in batches if necessary, until golden brown with lightly crisp edges (about 1 minute per side).

- Serve warm, topped with the lemon curd or marmalade and powdered sugar, if desired.

SERVES 2 TO 3

I'M NOT JEALOUS JAMBALAYA

MPB

If I'm scrolling through my Facebook feed and I see a girl with a similar sense of humor, style, or career who has achieved some sort of success, I immediately become thrilled! I usually call her or send her an extremely expensive orchid. You know that shirt I've been dying to buy but can't afford? I spend my entire paycheck on it and send it to her! Let's celebrate her. After I take four or five Klonopin, I like to send her the rest of the bottle. She should have everything I hold dear in my heart!

What next? Great! It's the girl who beat me out to play Miranda, whom I was named after, in *The Tempest* in high school. I'm definitely not still holding on to that. That would be totally

crazy! So now she's the editor in chief of the *New Yorker*. Good for her. I'm going to send her my paycheck because there's room for everyone and I need her to know just how not jealous I am. I'm not overcompensating. I'm just really excited!

Oh look, there's that hipster girl I interned with one summer, who is probably the best-dressed human I've ever seen on the planet! Oh, she sold her style blog, where she posts a daily photo of her big toe covered in lace, to Warren Buffett for $2 billion. Boy, does she deserve that money! I'm cutting off my toe and sending it to her in support because I really want her to know just how not jealous I am.

Oh, things are only getting better from here! The boy who, in sixth grade, told me I had absolutely no talent just published his first novel! It's being excerpted in the *Atlantic*. The girl who beat me out for the part in my high school play arranged it! And they're getting married. Taking them both out to an engagement dinner! I'm NOT JEALOUS AT ALL.

Let's get off the feed! Let's just click on people and start exploring! My ex-boyfriend is now dating an interior designer who literally just did the design scheme for heaven! She and his dog, who truly hated me, are getting along super well! This doesn't hurt me at all. I'm not weeping. I'm going to send them a gift certificate to this fancy human/doggy spa in Dubai that I heard about. They're going first class. I hope they enjoy it. They deserve it! And I'm not jealous.

I'm already feeling great about myself. Let's just go for it. Let's open the Instagram page of the ex-girlfriend of the guy I'm currently seeing. I'll now have to cancel my plans for the rest of the day, because I need at least four hours just to examine how skinny her legs are. God, they're skinny, but I'm not jealous. One might say she's ethereal. She makes her own dresses. Her glasses probably never fog up with sweat fumes and oils from her fingers. She probably never spends entire days vomiting from drink. Her friends all look just like her, but she's sort of the prettiest one. Why don't I have a group of friends who all look like me? Wow, their relationship looked so beautiful and easy, like the one John Mayer described in that song "Comfortable." Why did he break up with her? He's probably just seeing me in the interim until he gets back together with her. I'm probably not even good in bed. I don't want to stand in the way of anything important between them. I should do the good deed and end it with him now so he can go back to her. That would be the right thing to do. God, she's cool. God, her legs are skinny. I am not jealous. I am just suicidal.

Okay, I am jealous. I am jealous of the ethereal ex-girlfriend. I am jealous of the interior-designer current girlfriend. I'm jealous of my sixth-grade bully. I'm jealous of the style blogger. I'm jealous of the editor in chief of the *New Yorker*. What shall I do? Cry? Well, certainly. That's a given. Wallowing is my greatest skill. But if you have any problems with self-esteem, then going down that path will ruin you.

So instead of wallowing I will cook. I will tell myself I am not jealous by making jambalaya.

Anyhow, now you're done. Congrats! Do not sit alone eating a four-person serving of jambalaya. Invite some friends over. Any friends you can think of. Best-case scenario is people who make you feel good about yourself, but any bodies will do.

Set your table in the best way possible. Sit these friends down. Stage them. Serve them jambalaya. Take a photo and put it on the internet. I guarantee you will make at least one person jealous. That is the cycle. Good luck!

I'M NOT JEALOUS JAMBALAYA

INGREDIENTS

¼ cup extra-virgin olive oil

1 pound boneless, skinless chicken thighs

1 teaspoon salt, plus more to taste

1 teaspoon ground black pepper, plus more to taste

3 stalks celery, chopped fine

1 medium onion, chopped fine

1 green bell pepper, cored, seeded, and diced

1 pound andouille sausage, cut into ½-inch slices

2 cloves garlic, chopped

1 (15-ounce) can low-sodium chicken broth

1 (14-ounce) can crushed tomatoes, with their juice

1 cup uncooked long-grain rice (white or brown)

DIRECTIONS

- Heat the oil in a Dutch oven or large soup pot over medium-high heat.

- Season the chicken with the salt and pepper. Add to the pot and cook until golden brown, about 5 minutes per side.

- Remove the chicken from the pot and set aside to cool. When it is cool enough to handle, cut into ¾-inch cubes and set aside.

- Add the celery, onion, and bell pepper to the pot. Cook, stirring, for 5 minutes.

- Add the sausage and cook another 3 minutes.

- Add the garlic and cook 1 minute more.

- Stir in the broth, tomatoes, and ½ cup water. Bring to a boil.

- Add the rice and the cooked chicken and reduce heat to medium-low. Simmer for 5 minutes.

- Remove from heat and cover. Let stand until rice is tender and liquid is mostly absorbed, 30 to 35 minutes.

- Season with more salt and pepper if needed.

- Serve hot, ladled into bowls.

SERVES 3 TO 4

ALL MY FRIENDS ARE MARRIED MUD PIE

MPB

The change happens slowly. In the beginning, two of your friends have serious significant others. Then one of the couples breaks up because they realize they're not ready to take the next step, or they fear they'll have unattractive babies together. The other couple, though; the other couple gets engaged. And it's fun. It's your first friend getting married. Is she a little young? Sure. Would you get married at her age? No, definitely not, but you're not going to say anything. You're going to get the save-the-date, put it up on your fridge, and enjoy feeling like a grown-up as you browse her registry. *Look at me*, you'll think, *I'm, like, an adult.*

Then before you know it, the other friend who'd been dumped has found someone new. And even though it's only been six months, she's sure this is the guy. Jonathan was comfortable and sweet, but Raoul is adventurous. Now that she knows him she can't picture a life without him. They take hikes literally every morning. Can you believe it? Good for her, that's great. Just hope she knows she's paying for your ticket to her destination wedding because otherwise you can't go.

There are now two save-the-dates. Then out of the blue your high school boyfriend emails you the most beautiful save-the-date you've ever seen, for his engagement to his fiancé, Roger. This save-the-date is so gorgeous that you simply have to go to The Copy Shop to print it out and put it on your fridge. You tell yourself you want a more complete representation of all the different kinds of couples on your fridge.

Three is an okay number; you can handle three. Hell, you wanted three. But then you get another save-the-date from your coworker and you feel a strange compulsion to put it up on the fridge too. "The fridge needs diversity," you say. "The fridge holds up a mirror to the world."

Jump ahead two months. You've become obsessed. Your apartment is covered in save-the-dates and wedding invitations and you don't remember a life before people started getting engaged. You can't help yourself. You've even printed out engagement announcements from Facebook of people you don't know. Your closet is covered with Instagram photos of your favorite online weddings. You read a list of your favorite wedding hashtags before you go to sleep at night. This décor and behavior ensures that you will not miss any upcoming weddings, but also reminds you that you are stagnant. Other people are moving on and you are not.

Your behavior worsens. You go to spin class, and all the people you've been spinning with for the past four years are pregnant. You take Polaroids of them to hang up in your apartment. They're moving on and you want to be further reminded of your place in life as compared to

theirs. You imagine memories that never happened; you say, "I used to spend every Saturday having brunch with these girls and now it's all Lamaze class." You never spent one Saturday in your life with these girls, and you know that, come on.

Calm down. Stop hyperventilating in front of your Pinterest shrine to the English countryside wedding you may never have. You'll probably have it.

It's really hard when people around you are taking life steps that you either aren't ready for, don't want, or just haven't found the right person to take them with. When everyone around you is getting married, you can start to feel like some sort of child, or at least that's how I feel. I feel like I must be missing something. These people are moving on and I can't. I'm a kid. The truth is, though, while plenty of people I know are moving forward, at the age of twenty-eight, I'm not entirely ready to.

This is why I so very much love this mud pie. It encapsulates how I feel. On the outside, it looks like a totally grown-up, hard-to-make adult mud pie, but on the inside it's all ice cream and Oreos. Let's also be clear that everyone getting married doesn't necessarily have their shit together either. They're just getting married; we don't know what their other problems are. Everyone moves at their own pace, but when you feel like you're falling behind, make this dessert.

I suggest that while making this pie, you crush the Oreos with a bottle of red wine. Take a swig, crush, swig, and crush. You get it. Bring the pie to an engagement party and everyone will love it. We're all just pie on the outside and ice cream and Oreos on the inside.

Also, take down all those invitations on the walls. That's insane. You're crazy.

ALL MY FRIENDS ARE MARRIED MUD PIE

INGREDIENTS

1 pint chocolate ice cream

1 pint coffee ice cream

26 chocolate sandwich cookies (like Oreos, Hydrox, or Newman-O's), divided

2 tablespoons unsalted butter, melted

½ cup heavy whipping cream, or use the canned variety

pinch of sugar (optional)

½ cup chocolate fudge topping (be sure the container says "fudge topping" and not chocolate syrup)

¼ cup chopped walnuts or whole roasted peanuts (optional)

NOTE: You can swap out the ice cream for frozen yogurt and call this a light mud pie. It's great to keep in your freezer when you're jonesing for a dessert that's not too heavy.

DIRECTIONS

- Leave the ice cream in the refrigerator for at least 20 minutes, to soften it until it's spreadable.

- Meanwhile, finely crush 12 cookies. (You can do this in a food processor by pulsing until they're crushed, or by placing them in a zip-top bag and bashing the hell out of them with a rolling pin.)

- Combine the crushed cookies and the melted butter in a mixing bowl.

- Press the mixture firmly into the bottom of a 9-inch pie plate.

- Line the sides of the pie plate with the remaining 14 cookies, standing them on edge.

- Freeze for 10 minutes.

- Carefully spread the chocolate ice cream into the prepared crust.

- Spread the coffee ice cream over the chocolate layer.

- Freeze for at least 4 hours, until completely firm.

- If making your own whipped cream, place a metal or glass bowl into the freezer for 10 to 15 minutes, until very cold. Once cold, pour the heavy whipping cream and a pinch of sugar into a bowl. Use a whisk or an electric beater to whip the cream until stiff peaks are formed. Refrigerate until ready to use.

- Top the pie with fudge topping, nuts (if using), and the whipped cream.

- Slice and serve.

SERVES 6 TO 8

SUPER-SAD SATURDAY NIGHT SALMON

GLM

For the first three years I lived on my own, the idea of a weekend evening spent by myself was downright depressing. Why would I stay home when the opportunity to straighten my hair, put on sexy (read: uncomfortable) shoes, and make out with a stranger was available to me just about every weekend? *What if*, I would wonder, *my destiny lies beyond the bouncer skeptically allowing me in the door of this shitty club even though my fake ID says I was born in 1968? What if one of those cheesy strangers, who don't ever seem to mind that I've spilled vodka and cranberry down my too-tight top, is my true love? My* beshert, *as we say among Jews?*

But then one weekend in late spring, my Saturday-night plans fell through. I panicked briefly, calling everyone in my neighborhood to see if they might want to meet up instead, but nobody was around. Crestfallen, I called it. The night was over. Dead.

I washed off my makeup, changed into clean pajamas, and set about making dinner. I cooked a salmon fillet I'd bought earlier that week, topped it with a soy glaze and a fresh blood orange my roommate had been saving, and tossed together a quick side salad. I poured myself a glass of white wine, settled in with my dinner, and found a Molly Ringwald marathon on TBS. As I laughed and cried along with Molly, sipped my wine, and ate my dinner, it suddenly hit me: Saturday nights alone are actually kind of awesome. There was nobody to bother me since everyone was out getting drunk and making out with each other, and I had a rare opportunity to cook, eat, and veg out in peace. Best of all, I could cook and eat fish without offending anyone with the aroma. It was more relaxing than a deep-tissue massage (and much cheaper).

Since I met my husband, my weekend nights alone are fewer and further between. But a few times a year, he takes off for a weekend-long conference or goes out with his guy friends. I mope and pout and tell him how sad I am that I'll have to spend the weekend without him. Then I drop him off at the airport or the bar and head straight to my neighborhood grocery store, where I pick up ingredients for my very favorite solo meal. I cook dinner, run the bath and pour in a decadent amount of bubbles, grab a large glass of wine, and celebrate the joys of spoiling myself.

Because the secret of super-sad Saturday nights in is that they aren't very sad at all.

SUPER-SAD SATURDAY NIGHT SALMON

INGREDIENTS

1 tablespoon soy sauce

1 tablespoon brown sugar

2 cloves garlic, minced

1 (1-inch) piece of ginger, peeled and minced

1 blood orange, half zested and juiced, half sliced into thin rounds

1–2 teaspoons Asian chili sauce (depending on taste)

1 (4-ounce) fillet salmon, skin on

1 small bunch flat-leaf parsley, chopped, for garnish

DIRECTIONS

• Preheat the oven to 375°F.

• Combine soy sauce, brown sugar, garlic, ginger, blood orange zest and juice, and chili sauce in a large bowl. Whisk until well incorporated.

• Place salmon fillet flesh-side down in the marinade, gently pressing down to ensure that all of the fish is exposed to the marinade.

• Set in the refrigerator to marinate for 10 minutes.

• Place fillet skin-side down in a glass baking dish. Top with 2 or 3 slices of blood orange and bake for 10 to 12 minutes, or until fish is cooked to desired doneness.

• Garnish with parsley and serve.

SERVES 1

SCHADENFREUDE SUNDAE

MPB

When I was in fifth grade, I was doing poorly in history class. My teachers told my parents I needed a tutor, or that maybe I wasn't smart enough for the school. Determined to prove everyone wrong, I studied and got a 98% on the next exam. My closest friend and biggest competitor at the time, Hillary, got a 75%. Not only did I do well, but also I did better than she did! Hurray!

Her loss made my win all the sweeter, and thus, I realized how much fun it could be to take joy in other people's pain—how much other people's misfortunes could make me feel better about myself! Fifth-grade history class is my Marvel Universe evil villain origin story. (I like that it's small and relatable.)

In the years following, I continued to watch others experience sadness with delight. Sometimes I even *caused* the sadness! I told secrets! I excluded friends from my birthday parties! I talked shit constantly! I was not a very discreet or original villain. You might say I was just your average middle-school girl, but I promise I had way more style.

Unfortunately though, my behavior was forced to a crashing halt in seventh grade when my friends kicked me out of "the group" forever. This might also have had something to do with the fact that I was a very late bloomer and super afraid of boys, but anyway, I was taught to repress my criminal predilections because "girls shouldn't be mean" and "being mean isn't nice," and "don't you want friends, Miranda?"

So I went along, being nice, trying my best not to smile at other people's failures . . . until something changed that: social media. Suddenly, I was sweeping the internet for my enemies' most unfortunate moments and loving it. So I didn't get a promotion! Guess what: neither did this random idiot I maybe know from summer camp. *Muahhhaha.* I soon realized how much I had missed the evil-villain version of myself. I resented that she had been silenced and that I had been socialized to be kinder. I was the opposite of a *Frozen*, or a *Wicked*: I wanted to be mean for the sake of being mean once again. And now I had found a way: I could judge others without being judged for it from the privacy of my very own browser. I could even use an incognito web browser if I was feeling extra paranoid. Again, I'm probably not the most original villain, but again, I have pizzazz. When I'm embracing my truest Slytherin soul, I like to indulge completely and hold nothing back. I sit in my evil tower, laughing at people's Facebook stories, covered in stolen jewels, and eating this chocolate Sundae.* I deserve it, probably.

---

* You can enjoy this Sundae even if you are not evil, but why not go whole hog. Live your life, I say.

SCHADENFREUDE SUNDAE

INGREDIENTS

¼ cup salted hard pretzels (just about any kind works, including gluten-free)

2 tablespoons unsalted butter, melted

1 tablespoon sugar

2 large scoops vanilla (or your favorite flavor—you do you) ice cream (about 1 cup)

2 tablespoons store-bought hot fudge topping

2 tablespoons store-bought caramel topping

Whipped cream, for topping (out of a can is fine, or whip ¼ cup heavy cream with a pinch of sugar until soft peaks form)

DIRECTIONS

• Preheat the oven to 375°F.

• Line a rimmed baking sheet with parchment paper or aluminum foil.

• Place the pretzels, melted butter, and sugar in a bowl. Stir to combine.

• Spread the pretzels out on the lined baking sheet.

• Bake for 10 to 12 minutes, until the pretzels are toasted and caramelized.

• Remove from the oven and let cool completely.

• Scoop the ice cream into a bowl or glass.

• Microwave the hot fudge until heated (20 to 25 seconds should do it).

• Drizzle the hot fudge and the caramel over the ice cream.

• Sprinkle the pretzel mixture over the ice cream.

• Top with whipped cream.

• Eat while trolling Facebook and enjoying the fuck out of how much better your life is than your Facebook friends'.

SERVES 1

ABANDONMENT ISSUES APPLE PIE

MPB

Have you ever had a dream where you're in bed with someone, and they're spooning you, and then slowly they roll away from you until they completely let go, and then they're out of bed and putting on their pants and running away as fast as they can? Then you wake up (in the dream), and they're gone. And it's much more intense than if this were to happen in real life. (In real life, I don't need the spooning; I need to sleep.) But because this is a dream, it shows your true fear that this person is certainly, without a doubt, going to leave you?

Then you wake up (in real life), in a panic, positive that not only is this new lover going to leave you, but the mutual friend who set you two up will cease to be part of your life as well. Any humans you met while you two were together will also forget you exist. If for some reason they do remember your face, they won't even want to know you without your former partner. If they see you on the street, they will run in the opposite direction screaming. They will think you are a ghost, because to them, you have died. They will question everything because they thought they were the kind of person who didn't believe in ghosts.

You look at your phone and realize no one has texted you for an hour. You text thirty-five people. No one responds. Not even your parents are picking up their phones right now. You are completely alone.

This is my tipping point. When my hysteria is so cantankerous that I can only share it with my parents, and they don't pick up, that's when I know it's over. This is the apocalypse. That End of Days thing is real, maybe not for everyone, but for me.

How do you battle existential anxiety? You think wholesome thoughts. What is the most wholesome thing in the world you can think of? Apple pie. (Don't think of it in the gross *American Pie* way. Think of it in the Thanksgiving way.)

Get out of bed. Wash your face. Put clothes on. Call the friend who you know will be free, even though they're the friend you least like hanging out with, the friend who's even more desperate than you, who you talk shit about constantly but actually love. Tell them you are making an apple pie and watching your favorite movie. Tell them to be at your house in two hours.

When you are at the grocery store, strike up a conversation with a family. Smile at them. Feel warm feelings.

Go home. Start baking. I guarantee someone will have texted you back by this point. At the very least, you'll get a notification about your data usage, which will show that your service provider cares. Hopefully, you'll get a message from the lover in your dream, but if you don't, fear not! The pie is about to be done. Your friend is coming over, and you are going to enjoy it together and realize you are okay.

Watch a movie. Take a breath. You're not alone. At least, you know Gabi and Miranda are here with you.

Whoa, this got real sweet real fast. Love you? No, no, it's too soon for that. Be chill.

I'll just give you a classic xoxoxoxox.

ABANDONMENT ISSUES APPLE PIE

INGREDIENTS

For the crust

2 cups all-purpose flour, plus more for rolling

2 sticks unsalted butter (1 cup), chilled, cut into cubes

1 large pinch salt

3–4 tablespoons ice water

NOTE: We love to make piecrust from scratch, but you should feel free to use a store-bought crust if you prefer.

For the filling

3 pounds baking apples, like Golden Delicious, Cortland, or Fuji, cut into eighths

2 tablespoons freshly squeezed lemon juice

⅔ cup sugar, plus more for sprinkling on the pie

1 teaspoon ground cinnamon

4 tablespoons unsalted butter

To assemble and serve

1 large egg, lightly beaten

Vanilla ice cream or whipped cream (optional)

DIRECTIONS

Make the crust

- Put the flour, butter, and salt in the bowl of a food processor (or in a mixing bowl).

- Pulse until the mixture looks like coarse sand. If you're working by hand, use a pinching motion or two forks to incorporate the butter into the flour until there are no large lumps.

- Slowly pour in the ice water with the food processor running, 1 tablespoon at a time, just until the mixture comes together. For me, this usually means 3 to 4 tablespoons. Again, if you're doing this by hand, work in the water 1 tablespoon at a time until the mixture starts to stick together.

- Dump the dough onto a floured surface. With floured hands, pat it into a circle about 6 inches in diameter.

- Wrap the dough tightly in plastic wrap and refrigerate for at least 1 hour. (You may keep it frozen for up to 2 months. When you're ready to use it, defrost it in the fridge overnight.)

- After it has chilled, roll the dough out on a lightly floured surface. Roll into a disk approximately 11 to 12 inches across. Layer the dough between two pieces of parchment paper and refrigerate for at least 10 more minutes.

Make the filling

- Place the apple slices and the lemon juice in a medium bowl. Add the sugar and cinnamon and toss to combine completely.

- Melt the butter in a large frying pan over medium-high heat.

- Add the apples and cook, stirring frequently, until the sugar dissolves and the mixture begins to simmer, about 2 minutes.

- Cover the pan, reduce the heat to medium, and let cook until the apples soften and release most of their juices, about 10 minutes.

- Remove from heat and set aside.

Assemble the pie

- Preheat the oven to 375°F.

- Grease a 9-inch pie pan.

- Line the bottom of the pan with the dough. Trim the edges so they lie about ½ inch beyond the lip of the pan. Crimp as desired. (We usually do this with our fingers, but you could use a fork.)

- Put the apple filling in the crust, mounding it slightly in the center.

- Brush the exposed edges of the dough with the beaten egg.

- Refrigerate the uncooked pie for 15 minutes. (This helps ensure the crust will be as flaky as possible.)

- Place the pie plate on a rimmed baking sheet and bake for 35 to 40 minutes, or until the crust is golden brown.

- Let cool in the pan for at least 15 minutes before serving. Top with ice cream or whipped cream if desired.

SERVES 8

MISANTHROPIC MARSHMALLOW MELTDOWN

MPB

love people! Most of the time, I love people. At least 40 percent of the time, I'm super into people. But they're also the fucking worst. For example, at parties, a friend of mine always introduces herself with this really terrible joke about how we "met at a zombie orgy." I hate it. It's so bad. Every time she does it, I get down on the human race. How could anyone think that was an okay joke to make? I usually have to run out of the party and leave her to fend for herself.

I also love Twitter and Instagram and Snapchat and the internet in general. Of course, I am deeply ashamed of my social media overuse and I hate myself for it. What is texting anyway? Are we even communicating? Do I have friends? Are all my friends bots? It's unclear.

Finally, I love love. I love love so much, but I also want to enact a murder-suicide with some of my past romantic partners. I'd write their parents super-sweet notes, though, explaining why. They'd side with me.

Don't even get me started on the state of the world . . . (I mean, I'm sure there are tons of wars 'n' stuff happening right now. I definitely know about all of them. We don't need to get into specifics.)

So you see, like most people, I am dynamic. I both love and hate things. Usually I'm fairly balanced. Other times, though, all the evil parts conspire to turn me into a truly misanthropic monster. There's a curmudgeon down at the bottom of my soul. I try to keep her locked away so I can enjoy myself, but sometimes she just has to come out. (My friend's party joke will usually do the trick.) And I'm not talking about PMS here, I'm talking about really hating everyone and everything and seeing them for what they are: garbage from hell.

I know how I must deal with myself during these misanthropic meltdown times in order to come out of them alive. I must lock myself in my one-bedroom apartment and turn it into a cave. I turn off the lights and burn candles. I do not clean my home. I spill things, sticky things, and leave them. I step in them later. I listen to all the mean voices in my head. I don't pick up anyone's phone calls but my parents', and then only to start fights with them. Sometimes I tweet something dark, then I delete it because of how embarrassing it is and how dumb I think Twitter is. After that I'll try to erase my internet footprint as much as I can. I'll consider deleting my Snapchat account, but then stop myself. It's important to not be too rash during times like this. And my soul mate is probably on Snapchat.

I need to make myself okay enough to get back out into the world. And the only way to make this happen is to get so sick of myself that I start to miss people. Usually, this will happen after two to three days. Unless it's raining. If it's raining, I can stay in my misanthropic coma for five to seven days. If it continues to rain, like if I happen to be in India during monsoon season, it's likely I will never leave my home again. Usually, though, after three days I can't stand the sight of my vile apartment or my giant pores. I get worried everyone's forgotten about me and decide I must be okay again. There's also the pressure of, like, going to work and paying my bills and what have you.

But before I'm ready to rejoin the human race, I feel entitled to one final delicious meltdown snack. I may have to leave my cave to get the ingredients for this, but that's good. It will be good for me to see light at this point.

Anyhow, after all this, I'm fine. For at least a couple of weeks, or until the next time my friend makes that god-awful joke.

MISANTHROPIC MARSHMALLOW MELTDOWN

INGREDIENTS

2 cups semisweet chocolate chips (12 ounces)

1 (14-ounce) can sweetened condensed milk

1 (7-ounce) jar marshmallow crème (or 1½ cups miniature marshmallows, melted)

½ cup milk (any fat percentage)

1 teaspoon vanilla extract

2 cups fruit of your choice, cut into 1- to 2-inch pieces (we like strawberries and bananas)

2 cups regular marshmallows

2 cups store-bought angel food cake or pound cake, cubed

DIRECTIONS

• In a heavy-bottomed saucepan over medium heat, combine the chocolate chips, condensed milk, marshmallow crème or marshmallows, milk, and vanilla, stirring until just melted.

• Whisk until smooth.

• Transfer to a fondue pot and keep warm (or just eat standing over the stove like the hot mess you feel like right now).

• Serve with fruits, marshmallows, and cake pieces and skewers for dipping.

SERVES 6 TO 8

FUCK IT, LET'S JUST GET STONED NACHOS

GLM & MPB

h, fuck it. Fuck it all. Let's just get stoned.

INGREDIENTS

- 6 cups tortilla chips (note: this is a great way to use up almost-stale tortilla chips)
- 1 (15-ounce) can black or pinto beans, drained and rinsed
- 3 cups shredded cheddar or jack cheese
- 1 green jalapeño pepper, seeded and sliced (leave the seeds intact if you really like spicy), or 1 (4-ounce) can chopped green chilies
- 2 avocados, diced
- 1 green onion, diced
- 2 roma tomatoes, cored and diced, or cherry/grape tomatoes, halved
- 1 small bunch cilantro, chopped
- 1 (4-ounce) can sliced black olives (optional)
- ½ cup sour cream (optional)

DIRECTIONS

- Preheat the oven to 375°F.

- Spread the chips over an ungreased, foil-lined baking sheet. Scatter the beans over the chips. Cover with the shredded cheese and bake for 10 to 12 minutes, or until cheese is melted and bubbly.

- Top the baked nachos with jalapeño or green chilies, avocado, onion, tomato, cilantro, olives, and sour cream.

- Serve immediately, with small plates, so people can serve themselves. Or just put the pan out and dive in, man.

SERVES 4

CHAPTER 3

Deliver Us from Delivery

A good friend of mine, *The Mindy Project* writer Chris Schleicher, prides himself on being forever young. He thinks cooking is for old people and that by doing it he will prematurely age himself. And he can't take ANY risks. Starting to cook may end my friendship with Chris, but you know what they say: The more books you write, the fewer friends you need. Heh-heh. Anyhow, I think Chris might be wrong.

You are not a traitor to your generation if you learn to cook. In this chapter, we will show you how to make at home all the things you have become accustomed to buying or having delivered straight to your door in your modern life. Sorry, Chris. I am cooking and keeping my youth forever. The cream I use before bed every night insists that I'm going to look ten by tomorrow morning.

Of course, I get his point of view, and at one time I even agreed with him. How could I not have? We can have everything we've ever desired, and more, delivered right to our front doors. It is really a time for the hermit to shine. We're all basically a bunch of old Howard Hughses, ordering ice cream directly to our bedrooms. You can Postmates, you can Seamless, you can Eat24; you can even have a full romantic meal (plus the date) delivered to your home. "Just because you *can* do something doesn't mean you *should*" is a thing someone once said. "Taking the easy way out is not always the best thing" is another thing I heard. This is a lesson we millennials have to learn, in all aspects of our life. It is a lesson I struggle with every day. Instant gratification isn't fast enough for me. I don't even want to have sex. I just want to have already had the most amazing orgasm of my life without even knowing it happened. I also basically don't want to do anything. I just want to be really rich and happy and fulfilled without working through any of my shit or trying at all. This has not yet worked for me, so I'm trying to change.

Perhaps if we make our own pizza at home, we'll stop taking the easy way out in other parts of our life as well. We'll start in the kitchen and work our way out. We'll stop using our phones. We'll become connected people again. We'll leave our houses to get those massages we REALLY need. Or maybe we can't change, and we're all just destined to sit alone in a room with our phones forever. This would be fine. I love my phone more than my family, more than myself, more than anything or anyone. I miss my phone. I have to go. I haven't kissed my phone yet today. I'm worried it doesn't know how much I love it.

I'll leave you with this: Think of all the Instagram and Snapchat material you will get from cooking. Think of the likes! Think of the validation! Isn't that worth cooking for? Does a beautifully filtered selfie with a homemade gingerbread latte posted to the internet with a winning caption sound like it comes from some old fart? Not to me, it doesn't. It sounds like it comes from a young, cool hottie like yourself.

Honestly, at this point I feel like a gluttonous monster when I take out instead of cooking in. I look forward to coming home and making dinner. It makes me feel like a person—but still a cool person. —MPB

FRIED BRAIN FRIED RICE

MPB

Hey, hungover buddy,

Are you sprawled out on the couch about to order food? Stop! You can make it yourself! I promise. Give me a chance. Read this story, and if afterward you still think you have to take out, then do it. All right.

Did you accept the challenge? Cool. Let's get started.

. . .

"Sleeping with your best friend *never* works," we hear and then do it anyway because we need to take our chances. We need to feel alive. We need to get it out of our systems. We need to long-con our best friends into dating us. It always works!

Anyhow, I did it. I slept with my best guy friend and it was a bad idea. Some time afterward, when he and I were hashing out the state of our "friendship," which I of course now thought was more than a friendship, he told me he'd never wanted to sleep with me in the first place. He said I had pushed him into doing it and—get ready for this—he had felt like he "had to do it." He should be so fucking lucky. I'd never been so hurt in my life. (That's not true, but I was really hurt.) I was hurt enough to get ridiculously wasted that night.

I hadn't eaten anything during the day, because of anxiety, and hurt, and bad twenty-five-year-old eating habits. Oh, and it was Halloween. I dressed up as "your nightmare ex-girlfriend," wearing a giant sweatshirt and a slip and carrying a fake bloody knife around. I also had a hilarious box of ice cream with me all night as a prop. It melted all over my outfit until I stuck it in someone's sink and ran away. I drank everything you could possibly drink. I drank it all. I made friends with a group of cool-looking people at the one party I was invited to and accompanied them to four other parties. I drank more. I blabbed my entire story to them. They felt sorry for me. They helped me drink more. They wanted to find me people to make out with. At one of the five parties, there was guaranteed to be someone to make out with.

But there was a problem. I felt vomit rising. I wasn't going to "boot and rally." I had to get the fuck out of this fifth party. I got in an Uber and did my best to keep the vomit down, but I couldn't. I threw up all over that car. I didn't understand why the driver wouldn't pull over and let me out. He seemed to know just how quickly I needed to get home. He felt for me! What a nice guy!

The next morning, I woke up to about eighteen where are you / want to come over texts from unrecognizable numbers, and also to the worst hangover of my entire life. I suffer from a disease called vomitosis, which is something I made up: it just means I have really bad hangovers. That day will go down in vomitosis history. I couldn't keep anything down. Anything. Sweating, I drove to the urgent care clinic in my neighborhood to see if they could stick an I.V. in me. (I had seen this happen once on *Grey's Anatomy*.) The clinic couldn't help me, so I did something shameful. I did the most self-indulgent thing I'd ever done. I called The I.V. Doc. This is an on-demand nurse service for Hollywood celebs that sends someone to your house to stick a bag in you and rid you of your dehydration and nausea. It costs $200 and up, but I felt I had to do it. I'd been through vomitosis before and knew there was no end in hangover sight.

A few hours later, a sweet nurse I'd paid to take care of me after I had hurt myself physically because a boy had hurt me emotionally arrived. I will not hide from you how happy I was to be nurtured and taken care of in that moment, no matter the price.

After my nurse / new mom left, I was at last ready to eat. On hungover days I always treat myself to delivery. Mulling over what to eat, I checked my email and finally saw my Uber bill. The cab had also been $200. That's why the driver didn't stop and pull over; he was making bank off my vomitosis! He didn't really care about me! I would never have ordered the I.V. had I known how much the cab had been. You might say I should have checked the bill earlier and was probably avoiding it on purpose, and you might be right.

My hangover had now cost me $400-plus. This was the most expensive hangover of my life. I had spent my full hangover budget and much more. There was no way I could afford takeout now, at least not without feeling incredibly guilty. And I had also already spent my guilt budget for the month!

I didn't want to make pasta, though, or just eat toast. I wanted my regular hangover food. I had been through so much! So with the strength given to me by Debbie, The I.V. Doc, I went to the grocery store, bought the ingredients, and made fried rice for myself. This is a true tale of honor, I know.

There would be no taking out for a while after this night. There would be no buying anything at all, really, for a while after this night. I had a lot to save up. Still, the evening taught me a couple of very important things. First, it showed me that I definitely have a drinking problem and I should probably take care of that. Second, and more important, it showed me that it is possible to make your own hangover food. You can make fried rice. It's not that hard. And you should, because you've got to save your money. You never know when you're gonna vomit out $400.

Also, I slept with the guy again two weeks later. Now, we're married, except we're not at all and I'm lying.

. . .

Okay. The story is over. You are now free to take out if you so choose. I fully support you either way. I'm sending lots of love. I'm with you in spirit as your I.V. Doc, giving you an I.V. and antinausea medication, and also a kiss.

FRIED BRAIN FRIED RICE

INGREDIENTS

2 tablespoons coconut, canola, or other vegetable oil, divided

3 eggs, lightly beaten

1 tablespoon peeled, grated ginger

1 medium carrot, diced

4 ounces cooked ham or tofu, diced

4 white mushrooms, chopped

1 cup frozen peas

3 cups cooked white or brown rice (ideally a day old—this is a great use for leftovers)

2 tablespoons soy sauce

Salt and pepper

1 teaspoon toasted sesame oil

2 green onions, sliced

½ red bell pepper, diced

Hot sauce or sriracha (optional)

DIRECTIONS

• Heat a large frying pan over high heat and add 1 tablespoon of the oil.

• Add the eggs and scramble with a spatula, then set aside on a plate.

• Add the remaining 1 tablespoon oil to the frying pan. Add the ginger and cook for 30 seconds.

• Add the carrot and cook for 1 minute more, stirring occasionally.

• Add the ham or tofu and mushrooms and cook for 2 minutes.

• Add the peas and the cooked rice and toss together.

• Return the cooked egg to the frying pan.

• Season the mixture with the soy sauce and salt and pepper to taste.

• Add the sesame oil and stir to mix.

• Check the seasoning and add salt and pepper to taste.

• Garnish with green onions and red bell pepper and serve immediately, with hot sauce or sriracha if desired.

SERVES 2

A PAD (THAI) OF ONE'S OWN

GLM

This story is about a time when my lack of funds overpowered my ability to be a feminist. I'm not proud.

See, when you're young and hungry, like I was at age twenty, you sometimes accept dinner dates you might not otherwise go on. The promise of a restaurant is worth the two hours (an hour if you eat fast) of shitty small talk. It was particularly worth it for flat-broke college me (and my concept of independence had not yet fully formed).

There was a real dirtbag in my poli-sci class, Dieter (obviously not his real name . . . come on). I was almost positive he cheated off my midterm. So you can imagine my surprise when one day, apropos of nothing, he asked me out to dinner. (Sidebar: This was college. Who asks anyone out to dinner?) Under normal circumstances I wouldn't have gone, but again, I was poor (and also I was the only reason he passed that midterm). Plus, when you're young and an asshole is nice to you, you're so caught off guard and excited that you basically lose all control. (This has been my experience.)

At dinner, the waiter came over, and Dieter (isn't Dieter a fun name?) ordered for me without even asking what I wanted. I was shocked. My progressive Northern California upbringing had never put me in contact with this kind of backward "chivalry." I froze. I went along with it and ate the meal, but hated it and myself. There was a salty-sweet pad Thai on the menu that I had been dying to order, but Dieter had decided that, that night, I would be sharing his steamed chicken and brown rice.

I vowed to never let this happen again. I wasn't going to apologize for what I wanted to order.

Walking home afterward (alone—no nookie for Dieter, duh), I knew I should have stayed home and made my own pad Thai and retained my integrity. Now I make this as a reminder to always put myself first, and also because I like it, and it's easy and cheap.

A PAD (THAI) OF ONE'S OWN

INGREDIENTS

14 ounces dried rice noodles

2 cloves garlic, minced

1 (1-inch) piece of ginger, peeled and minced

3 tablespoons soy sauce

2 tablespoons brown sugar

Asian chili sauce (more or less to taste)

2 limes: 1 juiced, 1 cut into wedges

2 tablespoons coconut, canola, or other vegetable oil

2 (6-ounce) boneless, skinless chicken thighs (or tofu), cut into 1-inch cubes

1 small white onion, sliced thin

2 eggs, lightly beaten

2 cups mung bean sprouts

2 carrots, grated

1 small bunch cilantro, chopped

1 small bunch mint, chopped

4 green onions, sliced

¼ cup peanuts, crushed

DIRECTIONS

- Cook the rice noodles according to package directions in boiling water. Drain and rinse. Set aside.

- In a small bowl, whisk together the garlic, ginger, soy sauce, brown sugar, chili sauce, lime juice, and ½ cup warm water.

- Heat the vegetable oil in a large frying pan over high heat.

- Cook the chicken and white onion together for 5 minutes or until the chicken is cooked through.

- Add the eggs to the pan and scramble with a spatula. Continue to move them around as they cook and spread them throughout the pan.

- Add the cooked noodles and reduce heat to medium. Add the bean sprouts and carrots and toss well. Let cook for 1 minute.

- Add the soy sauce mixture and toss to coat.

- To serve, heap a pile of the pad Thai onto a plate or bowl. Top with the fresh herbs, green onions, crushed peanuts, and more chili sauce if desired. Garnish each plate or bowl with a lime wedge.

SERVES 2 TO 3

BETTER THAN TAKEOUT PIZZA

GLM

Pizza is the original delivery food, at least according to porn. I mean, have you ever seen a porn about a sexy soup delivery boy? (Disclaimer: I know there are all sorts of kinks out there, and I'm not in the business of judging, so if you're into soup porn, go get yours. But I think my point stands.)

While I will always love a hot slice at 2 a.m., after the bars close and I require something greasy to soak up all the booze (that's science, right?), when we're talking whole pies, I prefer to make my own pizza. After all, it's super simple (just dough, sauce, cheese, and toppings), and takes very little time to make (twenty minutes, tops, from start to finish—faster than it would take any delivery boy to show up at your door). But the most exciting thing, you piping hot pepperoni, you: not only is making pizza at home faster and cheaper than ordering it to be delivered, the result is also much tastier than the kind that comes in a box, and definitely more fun to make than the kind that comes frozen.

This is because when you make pizza at home, you get to eat it literally seconds after it comes out of the oven. (Okay, maybe it's prudent to give it a minute or two to cool down so you don't burn your tongue.) And unlike with delivery pizza, you get to completely control all the ingredients that go into it. It's a great way to turn leftovers into something new. Got leftover taco meat, cooked greens, corn, or tofu? Give them new life as a pizza topping! And it's a cheap, fun way to feed a lot of people. Want to throw a dinner party with hardly any work? Buy pizza dough, sauce, cheese, and toppings, and let people make their own pies. All you do is put everything out and do the baking.

Oh, and if you're still looking for porn to go along with your new pizza-obtaining method, just buy a pound of pizza dough and a gallon of tomato sauce and Google "sploshing."

NOTE: I got this pizza baking method from our literary agent, Richard Abate. It's the absolute best way to make charred-bottom, crispy New York–style pizza without a pizza oven.

BETTER THAN TAKEOUT PIZZA

INGREDIENTS

Flour for rolling and for pan

1 cup canned crushed tomatoes (preferably the fire-roasted variety)

2 cloves garlic, finely chopped

2 tablespoons extra-virgin olive oil

¼ cup packed fresh basil leaves, chopped fine, plus more for garnish

¼ teaspoon salt

¼ teaspoon pepper

1 pound prepared pizza dough (Whole Foods and Trader Joe's sell this for about $1.50)

1½ cups shredded mozzarella cheese

½ cup your favorite pizza topping (we love this one with tomatoes or red bell peppers and feta)

DIRECTIONS

- Preheat the oven to 500°F.

- Lightly flour a baking sheet or pizza pan and set aside.

- Drizzle a 16-inch sheet of aluminum foil with olive oil and set aside.

- In a small bowl, stir together the crushed tomatoes, garlic, 2 tablespoons of olive oil, basil, and the salt and pepper. Set aside.

- On a lightly floured surface, roll the pizza dough out into the desired shape. (I like to make mine oblong, since they fit on a baking sheet so nicely that way.)

- Transfer the dough to the oiled sheet of foil.

- Top with the sauce, cheese, toppings, and more basil.

- Place the dough-topped foil on the bottom of your oven. Not the bottom rack—the actual bottom. (I know it sounds weird. Trust me.)

- Let cook for 2 minutes, just until the bottom is very dark and crisp.

- Transfer to the prepared baking sheet and bake on a rack in the middle of the oven for 8 to 10 minutes, or until the crust is golden brown and the cheese is very bubbly.

- Let cool for a minute or so, then slice into wedges and serve.

SERVES 2 TO 3

LATE-NIGHT FAUX PHO

GLM

We all know that the ideal postparty situation is to leave with a group of friends, or your partner, or your partner for the night. Hop in a cab, listen to the tunes of the day, and make out in the backseat while holding back vomit and annoying your driver. What a dream. To be swaddled and deposited on your doorstep by the stork. We're not always that lucky (in fact, we're not often that lucky).

Once, during college, I was at a party in South Boston, which was about a thirty-minute drive from where I lived at the time. I was enjoying myself so much that I didn't realize each of my friends had slowly left without me. At the end of the night, I tried unsuccessfully to find a taxi. (Not that I could have afforded it. Taxis are for employed people.)

In the midst of a snowstorm, I had to walk home for two hours. In heels. I passed two police officers and they callously refused to give me a ride home. Apparently taking care of cold party girls is not part of the job. When I finally got home, I examined myself for frostbite. All fingers and toes were intact, my nose had started to thaw, and, though I was still drunk, I was significantly more alert than before I'd walked twelve miles in the snow. Oh, and I was starving.

I know many of you can relate to this: You made it home at the end of the night, maybe drunk, maybe sad, maybe freezing, maybe perilously close to vomiting, and definitely starving. Sure, it's great that you passed up a slice of late-night pizza, but what should you eat now?

On that particularly snowy night, starving and cold, I cooked up the scraps in my vegetable bin to make a soup that hardly resembled my favorite Vietnamese soup (essentially onion-skin broth with penne and some frozen spinach). Today, I love to make this quick version of a classic pho (the broth for traditional pho takes between 6 and 12 hours to cook properly). It's not quite the same as the classic, but it's pretty damn great.

LATE-NIGHT FAUX PHO

INGREDIENTS

1 tablespoon coconut oil or other vegetable oil

2 teaspoons Chinese five-spice powder

2 chicken legs (drumsticks and thighs), skin on

1 onion, skin on, quartered

5 cloves garlic, skin on, smashed

1 (1-inch) piece ginger, peeled and finely minced

2 stalks lemongrass, coarsely chopped (look for this in Asian grocery stores, or use lemongrass paste, available in tubes in the produce section)

Juice of 1 lemon

2½ tablespoons soy sauce, plus more to taste

2 tablespoons Asian fish sauce or soy sauce/tamari

1 tablespoon honey

2 teaspoons Asian chili sauce, plus more to taste

½ teaspoon pepper

8 ounces rice vermicelli

Optional garnishes: fresh cilantro, sliced jalapeño, sliced green onions, hoisin sauce, lemon wedges, mung bean sprouts

DIRECTIONS

- Heat the oil in a large soup pot over medium-high heat.

- Add the Chinese five-spice powder and cook, stirring constantly, for 1 minute.

- Add the chicken legs and brown on both sides, about 3 minutes per side.

- Add the onion, garlic, ginger, lemongrass, lemon juice, soy sauce, fish sauce, honey, chili sauce, pepper, and 2½ quarts of water.

- Cover and bring to a boil, then reduce to a simmer. Allow to simmer for 10 to 12 minutes, or until the chicken is cooked through.

- Once the chicken is fully cooked, fish it out using tongs and run under cold water to cool it down.

- Slide the skin off the chicken pieces, and use a fork or your fingers to remove the tender meat from the bones, reserving the bones, skin, and gristle.

- Return the bones, skin, and gristle to the pot, cover, and simmer for another 45 minutes.

- Strain the broth and return to its pot. Discard the solids.

- Taste for seasoning and adjust as necessary.

- Cook the rice vermicelli according to package directions. Drain and rinse. Set aside.

- To serve, divide the noodles between bowls and use a ladle to portion broth over the noodles.

- Divide the chicken pieces between the bowls, top with any of the optional garnishes, and serve immediately.

SERVES 4

NOT-SO-BASIC BITCH BEVERAGES: THE LATTE IN ITS MANY FORMS

MPB

'm quite certain the slang term *basic* will be in use until the end of time, but just in case it's not, and you're reading this book in the year 3022, let's define it. A basic girl is basic because she likes the same things as everyone else. She's not original. She follows the crowd and doesn't have any original opinions of her own. Some famous fictional basics might be Jane Bennet in *Pride and Prejudice*, Amy from *Little Women*, and even Charlotte York Goldenblatt from *Sex and the City*. Your typical basic was probably in a sorority. She loves astrology, *Us Weekly*, and giant sunglasses. Most famously, she adores pumpkin spice lattes.

For a large part of my life, even before the term for it was coined, I thought being considered basic would be the worst possible thing on the planet. I'm not basic at all. I'm confident saying that.

I do love some basic shit, though. In the past this would have embarrassed me. I thought the fact that I could recite every single line from every single episode of *Sex and the City* would make people think I was lame. Now, I think it's the coolest thing about me. You can be both basic and not basic at the same time. You can love some shit that basic girls love and still be complex. Let's not forget the intense pain Charlotte York Goldenblatt experienced in her life, or just how long Jane had to wait for Mr. Bingley to propose. Amy was kind of a bitch; I don't have anything nice to say about her. Also, these are the most basic references on earth, but we have to live our lives, and take our selfies, and have some fun.

But if you are still slightly insecure about your level of basic behavior, we're going to take any guilt away from it to help you out. We're going to show you how to make a pumpkin spice latte in the comfort of your own home! So no one sees. You can be a secret basic! My favorite kind of basic.

That said, if you make your own pumpkin spice latte, you're inherently not basic because making your own latte is cool as shit, and really impressive.

But be basic if you want to be. There's nothing wrong with it.

NOT-SO-BASIC BITCH BEVERAGES

INGREDIENTS

3 tablespoons strong ground coffee

⅔ cup water

⅔ cup milk (any fat percentage, or nondairy)

LATTE DIRECTIONS

- Brew the coffee with the water in a regular coffeemaker, French press, or drip cone.

- Pour the cold milk into a microwave-safe bowl, the edges of which should come up a bit higher than the milk.

- Tilt the bowl slightly, so that the milk is gathered more toward one side. Using a wire whisk, quickly and vigorously whisk the milk in the bowl for 2 to 2½ minutes. If the milk is not frothy after 2½ minutes, continue whisking an additional 30 to 60 seconds. The milk should be very frothy at this point.

- Microwave the milk in the bowl on high for 8 to 10 seconds. It should puff into a high foam immediately.

- To serve the latte, pour the hot coffee into a mug and top with the hot milk, spooning the thick foam on top. Serve immediately.

VANILLA LATTE: Whisk together a few drops of vanilla extract and 2 teaspoons honey or agave nectar to make a vanilla syrup. Whisk the syrup into the hot brewed coffee before adding the milk and foam.

PUMPKIN SPICE LATTE: Whisk together ¼ teaspoon pumpkin pie spice and 2 teaspoons honey or agave nectar to make a pumpkin spice syrup. Whisk the syrup into the hot brewed coffee before adding the milk and foam. Top the latte with a dash of pumpkin pie spice, fresh cinnamon, or nutmeg.

GREEN TEA LATTE: Instead of coffee, brew a strong cup of matcha green tea according to package directions. Sweeten as desired. Continue with the directions as written, replacing the brewed coffee with the tea. Top the latte with a sprinkle of the matcha powder, if desired.

CARAMEL MACCHIATO: Whisk 2 teaspoons caramel syrup (like the kind you would use to top ice cream) into the hot brewed coffee before adding the milk and foam, then top the latte with a drizzle of caramel syrup, if desired.

SERVES 1

SUSHI YOU CAN ACTUALLY MAKE, WE SWEAR

MPB

So, when Gabi suggested a maki roll recipe for this chapter, I shot her down. "Sushi?" I said. "Come on, you're being insane. We can teach them to fry rice. We can tell them to make pies when they're feeling down. We can even implore them to spend their hard-earned cash on a food processor. But no one's making sushi."

"It's expensive to order out for it all the time," Gabi argued.

"Yeah, yeah, yeah," I said, "tell it to Judge Judy; you can always find a cheap enough place to get your sodium fix."

So Gabi challenged me to make sushi on my own, and this is what I have to say: We were all told we could do whatever we wanted to in this world. That's not true, but you can do some pretty hard things, and making sushi isn't even one of them. It's, like, super easy.

Of course, at first, as is the case with any large endeavor, you are scared. You look in the mirror and think: *How did I get myself into this? I just want to lie in bed and order out, or maybe go to rehab.* Then you Gchat with a friend for five hours, you get yourself out of bed, and slowly you begin.

You go to the grocery store. You look at the email you sent to yourself with all the ingredients. You realize it was lost in the cloud and you only have 17 percent battery left. You call your friend and ask her to take a picture of the recipe for you (because obviously she has this book too. You all do. It's your bible). She's not home, but her ex-boyfriend is at her apartment picking up his stuff: "You can call him and ask if you want to." You do this because you left the house and it's really only a minor obstacle and secretly you think the breakup is totally her fault.

After you get the recipe from him, you move on. You only have 14 percent battery at this point, so you must be efficient and quick. Your adrenaline kicks in. You get the easy stuff first: carrots, cucumber, and avocado. Then you rush to get the rice. You feel like a badass when you ask the salesperson where the nori seaweed is. They think: *Who is this person buying seaweed? She must be so legit.* You feel legit. Your overall confidence is rising. You even made a lifelong friend with the fishmonger when you asked him for sashimi-grade yellowfin tuna. Shared experience creates lasting bonds, remember, but don't get too cocky. You only have 4 percent battery and you've got to use Apple Pay to check out because you forgot your wallet at home. (Another

lesson here: Writing ingredients down is not that bad of an idea. You never know when your phone might die. Grocery lists are very vintage.)

You get home. You make the rice. You cool it and spread it out onto the seaweed, then you add the fish and other fixings. I suggest grabbing some edamame and Sapporo to snack on while doing this. Soon you're ready to roll it all up. And, wait, then you're done. It's so easy! It's like probably one of the easiest recipes in the book. So Gabi was right: any hot mess can make sushi.

SUSHI YOU CAN ACTUALLY MAKE, WE SWEAR

INGREDIENTS

1 cup sushi rice, cooked according to package directions and cooled to room temperature

1 tablespoon rice vinegar

8 ounces sashimi-grade yellowfin tuna (or other sashimi-grade fish—look for sales at your local fishmonger)

6 sheets toasted nori seaweed (usually located near the soy sauce in well-stocked supermarkets)

1 ripe avocado, sliced

1 carrot, peeled and thinly sliced lengthwise

½ cucumber, peeled and thinly sliced lengthwise

Sesame seeds, for garnish

Soy sauce, wasabi, lemon, and pickled ginger, for serving

DIRECTIONS

• Drizzle the rice vinegar over the rice. Set aside.

• Slice the tuna into strips about the length and width of your finger (gross, we know). Set aside.

• Place a sheet of nori shiny-side down on a clean cutting board or sushi mat. Wet your hands completely and scoop up a handful of rice. Starting at the bottom of the nori, press an even layer of rice three-quarters of the way up. (Leave the top quarter of the nori bare. This will make for easier rolling.)

• Arrange 1 or 2 pieces of tuna and slices of the avocado, carrot, and cucumber in an even line at the bottom of the nori sheet, on top of the rice layer.

• Roll the nori tightly, encasing the tuna and vegetables. Use a little water to seal the end, if necessary. If you have a sushi mat, you can use it to roll the sushi at this point.

• Repeat with remaining nori, rice, tuna, and vegetables.

• Slice each long roll into 1-inch or 1½-inch pieces. Sprinkle lightly with sesame seeds.

• Serve with soy sauce, wasabi, lemon, and pickled ginger.

MAKES ABOUT 30 PIECES OF SUSHI

DIY FRO-YO

GLM

There's this thing that happens to me every single Sunday afternoon, like clockwork, sometime around 2 p.m., after I've had too much coffee and my hangover is just starting to wear off: I get an absolutely incurable craving for fro-yo. I don't know why, exactly—probably because at that point in the day, I've watched five hours of cat gifs, and my mouth is dry and has a bitter taste from all the coffee and the feline internet cuteness.

But there's another problem, which makes this craving more than a danger to my thighs and wallet: at this time on any given Sunday, I'm almost certainly still in my pajamas and suffering from an intense need to also lie in bed or on the couch and binge-watch bad reality television. I need frozen yogurt, and yet I am paralyzed by inertia and whatever is on Bravo (did you know that network used to show OPERA?!).

Since I am certain you also suffer from your own version of yogurt/reality paralysis, I would like to offer a solution: make fro-yo at home. Yes, really.

I usually make this with frozen strawberries, because I almost always have a bag of them in my freezer, but frozen mango, raspberries, pineapple, or blueberries are all delicious.

INGREDIENTS

16 ounces frozen strawberries (a 1-pound bag)

1 cup Greek yogurt (any fat percentage)

1 tablespoon honey or agave nectar

DIRECTIONS

- Combine the strawberries, yogurt, and honey or agave nectar in a food processor.

- Puree until the mixture resembles a thick smoothie.

- Scrape the mixture into a bowl or plastic container with a fitted lid.

- Cover tightly and place in the freezer until firm, about 2 hours.

- Scoop into bowls and serve immediately.

- The frozen yogurt will keep for up to 2 weeks in an airtight container in the freezer.

SERVES 2

EGG McMADE-IT-MYSELF SANDWICH

GLM & MPB

Wanna know why you're slumping over your desk at 11 a.m., unable to focus, desperately craving the cool, smooth respite of your pillow? Easy: You skipped breakfast. Or, to be more specific, you skipped breakfast with protein. Protein is amazing because it keeps you full and satisfied for longer than carbohydrates alone (a fact you've no doubt been hit over the head with by women's magazines and yogurt companies since

you learned to read and/or eat yogurt), and it's good for your brain, which helps you avoid that midmorning crash.

While we love a leisurely omelet with toast and fruit on the weekends, on weekday mornings, it's all about the portable breakfast. Enter our spin on the iconic New York City breakfast (the egg and cheese roll): the egg, cheese, and avocado.

A thick smear of avocado not only adds moisture but also gives the sandwich a good dose of heart-healthy fat, which helps keep you full even longer. We top the egg with a touch of cheese, but if you're avoiding dairy, feel free to skip it, or substitute extra avocado.

INGREDIENTS

1 English muffin, split (or use your favorite bread, roll, or a bagel, and yes, gluten-free ones work just fine)

1 tablespoon butter or extra-virgin olive oil

1 large egg

⅛ cup shredded cheddar, jack, or mozzarella cheese

¼ large ripe avocado, sliced

Salt and pepper

Hot sauce

1 or 2 slices cooked bacon (optional)

DIRECTIONS

- Toast the English muffin on both sides and set aside.

- Heat the butter or olive oil in a nonstick frying pan over medium-high heat.

- Crack the egg into the pan and cook until the white has firmed and the yolk is still runny (or flip and cook until the yolk is firm, if you don't like runny eggs).

- Sprinkle the cheese on the bottom half of the English muffin.

- Spread the avocado on the top half of the English muffin.

- Place the egg on the bottom half of the English muffin and sprinkle with salt, pepper, and hot sauce to taste. Add the bacon, if using, and then put the second piece of muffin on top.

- Serve immediately, or wrap in foil or a paper towel and eat on the go.

SERVES 1

CHAPTER 4

Eating Clean, or Whatever

Well, we certainly couldn't write a cookbook called *Hot Mess Kitchen* and not have a chapter like this one. A lot of what makes me a hot mess is my weird flawed body image. So I'm going to get a little earnest right here and talk about that because it's important and this is a cookbook and it would feel very weird to leave it out.

Recently, I was looking at a photograph of myself at twelve years old, on the day of my sixth-grade graduation. I looked perfectly adorable, but I remember thinking I looked "a little bit fat." I didn't yet know to blame it on water weight, so I was devastated. This makes me sad, but I haven't changed. Years later, when someone commented on an Instagram post of me asking if I was Adele I cried for the rest of the day and canceled all my plans. Adele! I know. Feel free to hate me for this. Adele is the most beautiful human on the planet, but at the time being likened to anyone who wasn't negative pounds was a travesty to me. So next, I did the only rational thing I could: I got stoned and put myself into a lineup of differently weighted celebrities. I decided that on a scale from Lana Del Rey to Adele, I'd be Renée Zellweger as Bridget Jones. (Not the new one where she has a baby; Bridget Jones Classic.)

I've always taken it as gospel that if I gain a little weight or look a little fat in a photo, I should suffer for it. Noticing that I'm a little larger than usual is, for me, the easiest and fastest way to tear myself down. My jeans not fitting is a tangible sign I am worthless.

I think plenty of you can relate. If I had a dollar for every time a friend of mine texted me something like "I feel fat" or "I'm bloated" or "I just weighed myself and I'm never leaving my house again," I'd be richer than everyone you know who's invented an app, combined.

In the past, the pain of not looking like the me I want to look like has been too intense for me to go on a regular diet; I've always tried to fix the problem overnight. (Again, I'm sure plenty of you can relate.) In college, a week of taking Adderall could do the trick, but as I got older I couldn't do that to my body anymore. (Also, my Adderall tolerance went up and the appetite suppressant wasn't working anymore, so I would just be up all night eating bagels.) So instead, I would try to do a healthier version of that, which to me meant trying to "eat only turkey for two weeks," or ordering a juice cleanse or meal delivery service I couldn't afford. Remember when I told you how I'd bounced a bunch of rent checks? Well, ordering these kinds of things when you make close to minimum wage will help with that.

Now the old methods only sound exhausting. The main thing that will work for me is "eating clean," which I really just define as paying attention to what I eat, not going overboard, and cutting out some things that make me feel shitty. Eating clean doesn't necessarily solve my weight problem overnight, but it makes me feel a drop better about myself because at least I know I'm paying attention to my body.

Following are some of Gabi's and my favorite eating-clean-type recipes. Enjoy them when you're feeling shitty, or after a weekend of drinking, overindulging, or just plain old eating straight from the trash can. (You're lying if you say you've never eaten from the trash can. We've all eaten from the trash can.) We're not saying eat only the following foods. Mix them in with your other meals! We don't know anything! We're not doctors! WE ARE NOT doctors. Stop telling people we're doctors. We cannot afford to get sued right now. But honestly, Gabi and I love the following foods and they make us feel good, so hopefully they'll make you feel good too. Define "eating clean" on your own terms, or something.

Let's all just stop feeling shitty about our bodies. Imagine all the extra energy we'd have to feel good about ourselves if we did! Too hard to imagine? I agree. The thought scares me. Let's just cook.

Also, stop staring at that picture of yourself. I swear it was just taken from a really weird angle. You look really hot right now. —MPB

PALEO PAIN IN THE (ADMITTEDLY, WELL-TONED) BUTT CURRY

GLM

I have no problem with the Paleo diet, in its essence. To me, it makes a lot of sense: eat whole foods, don't fear healthy fats, and go easy on the carbs. (Okay, I know it's a tiny bit more complex than that.) It's the way people rhapsodize about it that I find annoying. Oh, really, you like to eat like they did in the Paleolithic era? Is that why you like unrefined coconut oil so much? Because the cavemen used so much of it? Did they have iPhones back then too? I don't remember ever hearing about mastodons meeting on Tinder.

I have pretty much zero patience for self-righteous Paleo eaters (or self-righteous eaters of any sort, really). Like, I'm thrilled that turning your back on grains and eating the way "our ancestors did" is helping you in so many ways (truly, I am!), but there is no reason to make your dining companions feel bad about the baked ziti they just ordered. You are not better than anyone at this table, no matter how much you talk about CrossFit.

As a cook and general avoider of conflict, my approach to dealing with this sort of baloney (not that Paleo dieters would ever eat a meat as processed as baloney) is to focus on food that is objectively delicious, no matter one's dietary restrictions. I want to distract everyone with eyes-rolling-back-in-your-head foodgasms so nobody talks about kettlebell exercises. This dish is my go-to for shutting people up: outrageously tasty, incidentally Paleo.

If you want to be like a real Paleo caveman/cavelady, kill the cow yourself and butcher it on your kitchen table (your roommates will be totally chill with this), and cut up the squash with a stick that you strapped a sharpened rock to. If you're a little more twenty-first century than that, do what I do and buy the meat cubed and the squash cut up in bags, near the other precut vegetables.

PALEO PAIN IN THE (ADMITTEDLY, WELL-TONED) BUTT CURRY

INGREDIENTS

For the curry

6 cups cubed butternut squash (cut it yourself or buy it precut)

1 tablespoon neutral oil, such as coconut or grapeseed

1 medium onion, cut into 1-inch pieces

3 cloves garlic, chopped

1 (1-inch) piece ginger, peeled and minced

½ pound cubed beef stew meat

1 (14-ounce) can coconut milk

1 tablespoon wheat-free tamari (soy sauce usually has wheat in it—if you're cooking for nonstrict Paleo followers, go ahead and use regular soy sauce)

2 teaspoons Thai red curry paste

2 teaspoons honey

1 red bell pepper, cored, seeded, and cut into 1-inch pieces

1 handful fresh cilantro, chopped

NOTE: If butternut squash is out of season, feel free to use scrubbed, cubed sweet potatoes.

For the cauliflower rice

1 head cauliflower, roughly chopped (no need to remove the inner core—just cut it up along with the florets)

1 tablespoon extra-virgin olive oil

3 cloves garlic, chopped

1 handful cilantro or parsley, chopped

¼ teaspoon salt

¼ teaspoon pepper

DIRECTIONS

Make the curry

- Preheat the oven to 375°F.

- Spread the squash out in an even layer on an ungreased baking sheet (use two if necessary) and roast for 35 to 40 minutes, just until the squash is tender when pricked with a fork.

- While the squash roasts, make the cauliflower rice (recipe follows). About 20 minutes before the squash is finished roasting, heat the oil over medium heat in a large frying pan (make sure it has a fitted lid—you'll need it later).

- Add the onion, garlic, and ginger and cook, stirring once or twice, for 2 minutes.

- Add the beef and brown lightly on all sides.

- Add the coconut milk, tamari, curry paste, and honey and stir well to make a creamy, pale red sauce.

- Add the bell pepper and stir well, then cover the pan with the fitted lid. Cook, covered, for about 15 minutes.

- Once the squash is done, carefully add it to the pan. Stir well and cover again. Cook for another 18 to 20 minutes, until the beef is very tender.

- Serve in bowls over cauliflower rice, topped with the chopped cilantro.

Make the cauliflower rice

- Place the cauliflower in a food processor and pulse until it resembles a fine grain. You may need to work in batches if your food processor is on the small side.

- Heat the olive oil in a large frying pan over medium-high heat.

- Add the garlic and cook for approximately 30 seconds, just until fragrant.

- Add the processed cauliflower and stir well to distribute the garlic.

- Cook for 7 to 8 minutes, or until the cauliflower is lightly browned in patches.

- Stir in the chopped cilantro or parsley as well as the salt and pepper.

SERVES 4

BASICALLY CARBLESS (NOT THAT WE CARE) CAULIFLOWER CRUST PIZZA

GLM

I don't believe in ruling out any foods. In my experience, as soon as you do that you're bound to fantasize of nothing but forbidden delicacies all day long, until you inevitably crack and eat whatever you swore you wouldn't on the kitchen floor at three o'clock in the morning. Rather, I like to make a practice of eating healthfully most of the time so that when I'm invited to a nine-course pasta dinner, a doughnut shop opening, or a cake tasting, I can freely partake without any guilt. An 85 percent virtuous / 15 percent decadent rule tends to keep me relatively sane.

I've found the key to staving off cravings when it's not quite time to indulge in that 15 percent is to replicate white, starchy, not-so-good-for-you foods with the king of vegetables, cauliflower.

It starts with about half a cauliflower, cut into florets (but if you live near a Trader Joe's that stocks cauliflower rice, you can use that). Through the magic of baking (plus some eggs, Parmesan, and salt), I turn it into a pizza crust that, while it doesn't taste exactly like regular pizza crust, comes pretty damn close.

I like to top this pizza very simply, since the crust is somewhat delicate—usually just sauce, cheese, and some greens or another vegetable, but I've made it with pepperoni, sausage, and fried eggs, all with good results.

INGREDIENTS

½ large cauliflower, cut into florets

2 eggs, lightly beaten

2 tablespoons extra-virgin olive oil, divided

½ cup grated Parmesan, plus more for topping the pizza

Pinch of salt

¼ cup sauce of your choice (tomato, pesto, romesco, etc.)

1 cup shredded mozzarella cheese

1–2 toppings of choice (we love sliced bell pepper, pepperoni, mushrooms, olives, and caramelized onions)

Fresh herbs—we like sliced basil and chopped parsley (optional)

Red chili flakes (optional)

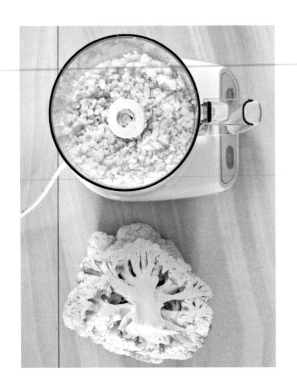

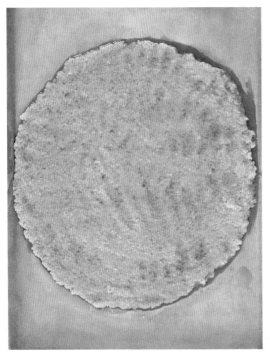
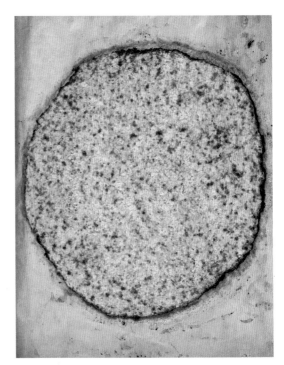

CAULIFLOWER CRUST PIZZA, continued

DIRECTIONS

- Preheat the oven to 400°F.

- Place the cauliflower florets in a food processor and puree until the mixture resembles ricotta cheese and each grain is about the size of a piece of couscous.

  TIP: If you can't seem to get the right consistency, or if a few whole florets remain after pureeing, try adding enough water to cover (usually about 2 cups) and puree as if you are making soup. When all the cauliflower has been completely processed, strain it in a fine-mesh strainer.

- Scrape the cauliflower into a microwave-safe bowl and microwave it on high for 5 minutes.

- Carefully scrape the microwaved cauliflower puree onto a clean dish towel.

- Very carefully (using a second towel if necessary to protect your hands) squeeze out as much liquid as possible. Get it as dry as you can.

- In a mixing bowl, combine the cauliflower, the eggs, 1 tablespoon of the olive oil, the Parmesan, and the salt. Mix together to make a thick batter.

- Line a baking sheet with parchment paper.

- Scrape the batter into the center of the parchment. Gather the batter into a ball shape.

- Wet your hands and carefully pat the batter into a circle, making it as thin as possible.

- Drizzle the cauliflower circle with the remaining 1 tablespoon of olive oil and use your hand or a pastry brush to spread it all over the circle.

- Bake for 30 minutes, or until the crust is nicely browned and a little crisp.

- Remove the crust from the oven, but leave the oven on.

- Place a piece of parchment paper over the top of the cooked crust.

- Carefully flip the whole thing so the bottom is facing up.

- Remove the top layer of parchment (what was previously the bottom layer).

- Top your pizza with sauce, cheese, and anything else you like. (I encourage you to go light on the toppings—the crust is sturdy but not as sturdy as conventional pizza crust.)

- Bake for 20 to 22 minutes more, until the cheese is browned and bubbly.

- Slice and serve, topping with fresh herbs and red chili flakes if desired.

SERVES 2

BETTER THAN YOUR $10 GREEN JUICE GREEN JUICE

MPB

've cheated on spelling tests. I've cheated in tennis matches. I've even cheated time (I look sixteen). But I have cheated on nothing more than I've cheated on juice cleanses. This hasn't stopped me from ordering them time and time again. I can't tell you how many juice cleanses I've ordered in my life, because I don't remember, because it's been so many. Even if I could remember, I wouldn't tell you because it's really, really fucking embarrassing.

"No, I can't go out to dinner because I'm on a juice cleanse," I'd tell a friend. Then I'd stay home and heat up the juice to make it "soup." That wouldn't work and I'd feel bad for myself and eat everything. I could never make it to dinner, but I could always make it to breakfast and sometimes lunch. Trying to drink eight juices a day does not work for me, but substituting one for a meal does work and usually makes me feel great.

While enjoying one or two green juices a day is a great idea, paying $400 for a diamond-encrusted pressed elixir is not. Half the time I'm only buying these beverages for their designer labels anyway. If you are like me, I suggest dumpster diving outside the chicest juice place in your neighborhood and stealing a bottle. After this, go home and carefully remove the label. Next, go to your local print shop and photocopy the label. Then make our juice, package it, stick your photocopied label on it, and sell it for less than the store would. You're eating healthy and starting a business. Is this a Ponzi scheme? I'm not sure. I don't know what a Ponzi scheme is. Anyhow, this plan is all in the name of eating well, and it's much more lucrative and easier to follow than an actual juice cleanse. Is this cheating? Who cares. I already told you I love cheating. Please enjoy both your juice and your money. Damn, we're giving you so much green with this recipe.

BETTER GREEN JUICE

INGREDIENTS

1 cup chopped mango (frozen is fine)

1 cup packed dinosaur kale leaves (the long, dark-green kind, not the curly kind)

1 cup packed spinach leaves

1 apple, cored and chopped

½ cup coconut water (or use regular water)

Some other favorite fruit/veg combinations

1 cup chopped pear, 2 cups spinach, juice of 1 lemon, ½ cup coconut water (or regular water)

1 cup chopped pineapple (frozen is fine), 1 cup kale, 1 cup spinach, juice of 1 lemon, ½ cup coconut water (or regular water)

1 cup chopped apple; 2 cups spinach; juice of 1 lemon; 2 stalks celery, chopped; ½ cup coconut water (or regular water)

DIRECTIONS

• If you have a Vitamix or other professional-grade blender, you can simply blend this until it's smooth (about 1 minute on the highest setting) and drink it as a smoothie.

• Alternately, puree as much as possible in a regular blender or food processor, and then strain, using a fine-mesh strainer, right into a drinking glass or jar.

• Drink immediately.

SERVES 1

COMMEMORATIVE KALE SALAD

GLM & MPB

We imagine some of you are going to use this book as a time capsule. It will be the way you remember your youth in years to come. Well, if you're reading this to your great-great-great-grandchildren, postdefrosting after being cryogenically frozen, then we think you must explain to them what kale meant in the 2000s. Kale meant so much to so many people. It meant a new vegetable to some, hope to others. It started off small

and then it was everywhere. It was a way of life and love. It was almost as important as brussels sprouts and bacon. Please tell your great-great-great-grandkids about brussels sprouts and bacon as well.

We certainly couldn't write an eating clean chapter without a salad, and we felt that salad had to be kale. This is a book for millennials (and millennials at heart) and kale has been our touchstone vegetable. Frankly, if we were to walk into a restaurant today that didn't have kale on the menu, we would run out screaming and report the place to the FDA. Even if kale's moment is over by the time this book comes out, then we commemorate it here. We hope your great-great-great-grandchildren like it as much as we have. Also, what's the vegetable in the current time? Please leave a note with each of our closest descendants to let us know. We'll probably still be frozen; neither of us is getting defrosted until at least 5022. Thanks so much.

COMMEMORATIVE KALE SALAD

INGREDIENTS

2 tablespoons raw pumpkin seeds

2 tablespoons apple cider vinegar or rice vinegar

1 tablespoon extra-virgin olive oil

A few drops honey (or stevia, if you're into that kind of thing)

¼ teaspoon salt

2 cups kale leaves, destemmed and sliced thin (about 1 medium bunch of kale)

½ cup shredded carrot (yes, you can totally buy it pre-shredded)

½ cup cherry tomatoes, halved

½ cup sliced cucumber (we never bother peeling them)

Sliced cooked chicken breast (see page 145) or tofu (see page 51) (optional)

Pepper

DIRECTIONS

• Heat a dry medium-size frying pan over medium-high heat.

• Spread the pumpkin seeds in a single layer in the frying pan and let toast for 1 to 2 minutes, shaking the pan around a few times to be sure they get toasted as evenly as possible. Remove from heat and set aside.

• Whisk together the vinegar, olive oil, honey or stevia, and salt.

• Put the kale in a large bowl and pour two-thirds of the vinegar dressing over them. Use your hands to toss (trust us, it's better than using tongs).

• Add the remaining vegetables to the kale mixture and toss with the remaining dressing to coat well.

• Transfer the salad to a serving bowl, if desired (or just leave it in the bowl you mixed in), and top with the toasted pumpkin seeds, chicken or tofu if using, and pepper to taste.

• Serve immediately.

SERVES 1

HOW TO COOK A CHICKEN BREAST THAT DOESN'T SUCK

MPB

I think chicken means a lot of different things to a lot of different people. To an average, functional eater, a chicken is a hearty piece of protein with which you can satiate your hunger. To a smokin' hot hunky rooster, a chicken is a lover and/or best friend with whom he has only a short amount of time to mate. But to me, a chicken is an existential matter. I was not raised in a home where pizza or burgers or fries were allowed. In fact, they were taboo, and if I asked for them at the dinner table, I would be stared at as though I'd committed some sort of serious war crime and death were imminent. "Grilled chicken salad, please," I'd say instead, and groan. This aversion has become ingrained in me and has continued into my adult life. I often want to be healthy, and chicken is a much more readily available item of healthy food than, say, fish, so I'm left ordering it basically every day for lunch. I think many women, and girls, and boys, and men, and most humans share this problem with me. We all order chicken salads all fucking day long. My life is just a series of grilled chicken salads, only some days the dressing is better than others. I just have to pray it's, like, a blue cheese dressing day. So how do we make every day a blue cheese dressing kind of day? We make chicken breasts that don't suck.

HOW TO COOK A CHICKEN BREAST THAT DOESN'T SUCK

INGREDIENTS

1 (3–4-ounce) boneless, skinless chicken breast

Salt and pepper

1 tablespoon extra-virgin olive oil, if cooking in a pan

Lemon (optional)

Fresh herbs (optional)

DIRECTIONS

- A boneless, skinless chicken breast is inconveniently shaped in that it is very thick at the top and tapers to a thin point. This makes it challenging to cook the thick part all the way through without completely drying out the thin part. To handle this, use a meat pounder (or a rolling pin, or even the bottom of a heavy jar or bottle) to pound the breast out so it's all about the same thickness. We like to cover the breast with waxed paper or plastic wrap before doing this to keep mess to a minimum.

- Season the breast on both sides with salt and pepper.

To cook the chicken on the stovetop

- Heat the oil over medium-high heat.

- Cook the chicken breast for 2 minutes without disturbing it (this will help the meat form a crust, which will both taste good and keep the inside juicy).

- Lower the heat and cover the pan or move the (ovenproof) pan into the oven (at 375°F). Cook for 3 to 4 minutes on each side.

To cook the chicken on a grill

- Heat the grill to medium-high.

- Place the chicken on the outer (less hot) part of the grill. Let cook for 7 to 8 minutes, flipping halfway through.

To finish and serve

- After grilling or pan-cooking, let the chicken rest for 2 to 3 minutes on a cutting board or plate before cutting into it. You want to retain all the meat's juices, and resting is a critical part of this.

- Top with a squeeze of fresh lemon juice and a sprinkle of herbs, if desired.

SERVES 1

SMUG SUPERIORITY SMOOTHIE BOWL

MPB

You know that really hot girl from your high school? The one who you were promised time and time again would grow up to be a hideous tree? Well, sorry, but she's still hot. I've seen her around in LA. And at first, I wanted to hate her for you. I really, really did. I fully had your back, but then, one day after spin class, she asked me to lunch. I was so caught off guard that I agreed.

She took me to this restaurant called Just Barely Food and ordered me a smoothie bowl. (I mean I paid for it, but she didn't even check with me. She was aggressive as hell.) I was shocked and angry when I found the meal delicious. Did I have to like this girl now? No, I didn't, but I definitely did have to make my own version of this bowl. And also, I'm sorry, but I kind of liked her too. She's nice now. Give her a chance.

INGREDIENTS

For the smoothie

½ cup chopped mango (frozen is fine)

½ cup packed dinosaur kale (the long, dark-green kind, not the curly kind), destemmed

1 cup packed spinach leaves

1 cup coconut water (or use regular water or your favorite juice)

For the toppings, use any of the following

½ cup fresh strawberries (or other fresh fruit), sliced

¼ cup granola

2 tablespoons shredded raw coconut

2 tablespoons raw pumpkin seeds (or your favorite raw or toasted nut or seed)

1–2 tablespoons your favorite nut butter

DIRECTIONS

• Blend the smoothie ingredients until smooth.

• Pour the smoothie into a bowl.

• Top the smoothie with the toppings of your choice.

• Eat, with a spoon, while looking as smug as possible.

SERVES 1

CHAPTER 5

Entertaining Your Enemies, Frenemies, and Friends

Nothing has the uncanny ability to make you feel inferior like going to a dinner party at the perfect home of your perfect friend, who seems to always have her shit together.

Where did this bitch get so much matching serving ware? you ask yourself as she effortlessly places a piece of perfectly cooked black cod with braised chard and rice pilaf on the expensive-looking plate in front of you. *How the hell did she find time to make dessert? Who the hell actually makes soufflés? Why isn't the kitchen a disaster? Why is her dress so clean? When did she have time to put on makeup? Maybe I shouldn't be friends with someone so perfect anymore! I could never have her over to my house! Aaaaahhhh!!!*

Okay. Breathe.

First of all, don't worry about this superhuman freak of nature. She and her Williams-Sonoma kitchen and Pottery Barn dining room have nothing to do with you and your slightly more . . . eclectic ones. Second, you should most definitely have her over to your house, along with four or five other people. This weekend. Because entertaining is the best way in the world to feel like you have your shit together, even when you most definitely do not.

There are a few reasons why this is true:

1. It feels good to feed other people. As a caterer, I learned an incredible principle of entertaining: People like to be fed, which means you can get away with simpler food. People are impressed by uncomplicated, straightforward food as long as someone else is making it. The act of placing homemade food in front of someone is like serving everything with a warm snuggle, and that creates a feel-good-feed-good cycle.

2. It forces you to clean up. Even if you're just tidying up, there's nothing like knowing a few people are coming over to get you to make your bed, take out the trash, and finally compost that plant you killed six months ago. Plus, if your guests are decent people, they'll help you do the dishes after the meal, which means you will be left with a gorgeously clean place and a clean kitchen.

3. When you provide the meal, it's appropriate to ask people to bring wine. And if there are a few bottles left over after dinner, they're yours to keep! I've built my entire wine cellar this way, one party at a time.

So why don't you give it a shot? In all the glory of your mismatched china, warped dining room table, ratty couch, and annoying roommates. Make a simple dish or four (this chapter has plenty of recipes to help you with that part), ask your friends to pick up the vino and some ice cream (yes, it's totally fine to outsource dessert, despite your friend's crazy soufflé-making habit), and serve food to the people you love, exactly as you are. We're pretty sure they'll love it, exactly as it is. —GLM

HOW TO THROW A FABULOUS DINNER PARTY WITHOUT HAVING AN ANXIETY ATTACK

To all the budding hosts and hostesses out there: Are you living up to your dinner party potential? Who cares? Listen up.

For as long as I can remember, throwing a chic dinner party with good food, conversation, and the mixing of friends has meant the ultimate in having-your-shit-together adulthood. I would hold this fabulous looming dinner party over my head and constantly threaten people with inviting them to it. I was the girl who cried entertaining. The beautiful dinner party I imagined would look like it was right out of a Woody Allen movie. I used it as a symbol, a symbol of something I could not attain. I wanted so badly to put on a long dress (you have to wear a long dress when entertaining at your home; it's written in stone), be my best self, and show everyone how fabulous I was, but for some reason I wouldn't let myself. I wasn't there yet.

I finally found an excuse to do it only when I started dating a guy who I thought would really, really appreciate it. He, like me, wanted to live his life like an indie movie. I thought this dinner party was the ticket to his heart. So with manic excitement on my side and my birthday to celebrate ahead, I set out to finally have the party of my dreams. This would be my night to end all nights. I would prove to myself that I could have this party and get myself a boyfriend to boot.

The day of the party arrived, and my heart rate was so high I had to leave work early. I couldn't concentrate on anything. My friend Sam picked me up to go to the supermarket. I was doing that cool codependent thing where I wouldn't let her leave my side. Sometimes you really have to love your girlfriends for what they do for you.

I burned my chicken and ended up having one delivered, but aside from that everything looked great. I rented a table and a set of chairs. I spent all my extra money for the month on this. I was pretending it was for my birthday, but it was for him. I didn't deserve my fabulous dinner party, but somehow he did.

An hour went by, and he didn't arrive. I took a Xanax. I had a drink. I had eight more. Another hour went by and finally, after weighing the feelings of the entire table, I decided to text him. He said he was "working late." I went berserk. The anxiety attack had ended, but the decision to get more wasted was still ahead. I eventually kicked everyone out, pretending the landlord had called to say it was too loud. I couldn't have them know I just didn't want to party. I was fucking devastated.

I woke up the next morning with a bucket next to me, feeling empty both emotionally and physically. There were birthday decorations and leftover wineglasses everywhere, but I refused to clean my apartment. I thought it was art-directed so perfectly for my mood that I wanted to keep it disgusting for as long as I could. I was so ashamed, but for the first time I understood the fact that you can't do things for other people; you can only do them for yourself. I was twenty-five and legitimately just understanding what this meant.

Eventually, I decided to throw another dinner party. I didn't aim as high as the first time. I didn't rent a table. I invited a group of friends, new and old, none of whom made me feel inferior, all people I felt comfortable around. And I told everyone what to bring. I was seeing a guy at the time, but I didn't invite him, because I knew if I had then it would have become all about him, and I needed it to not be. I needed it to be for myself and my friends, and to show myself that I could do it. Also, I've learned that you don't always have to do the most anxiety-provoking thing possible.

So I threw the party for myself, and it was lovely. The stakes were low. It was not my perfect Woody Allen dinner party, but I definitely think it could be featured in a super-low-budget indie movie. One party will not be everything. It will take many parties for me to be the kind of entertainer I want to be, but I will get there. And I will wear a long dress every single time. —MPB

JUST PUT IT IN A BOWL, OR NO-COOK APPETIZERS TO MAKE PEOPLE THINK YOU HAVE YOUR SHIT TOGETHER

MPB

Let's take a second to talk about bowls, and not just a set of six everyday white china bowls or mixing bowls or marijuana bowls. Let's talk about starting to collect cool, colorful bowls, because it's something I think you should do. The bowls, for example, that you buy at antiques fairs, or the one you agonize over on Etsy, and finally the ones you strategically steal from your favorite restaurants when you're drunk.

These bowls are going to be put to good use and are going to save you time and money. Most important, they are going to make you look chic and together as hell.

The best lesson I learned from my mother, a truly fabulous entertainer, is that when having a dinner party, or any kind of gathering, you should cover your apartment in bowls. Drown your guests in bowls. For someone like my mother, who also has, like, quiches and tarts for hors d'oeuvres, a bowl is just a special touch. The bowls are an example of a host going above and beyond to make sure there is not an instant during which one of her guests cannot satisfy an oral fixation. To us younger folks, foods in bowls become last-minute hors d'oeuvres. You're planning a home-cooked meal. You can't also be bothered to make home-cooked hors d'oeuvres. That said, the bowls still deliver the same atmosphere to a young person's party as they would to one of my mother's.

A guest walks into your house, grabs a handful of almonds, and immediately feels at home. They're in love with you and never leaving. They're just so happy there's food readily available! Do you have any super-awkward guests who you didn't want to invite but had to because of social politics? Talk to them about the bowls! Tell them the story of how you procured this bowl from a lion's mouth at a bazaar in Marrakech. (The stories don't have to be true. You didn't even want this person at your party.) Bowl snacks can be refilled all night long, but they look much nicer than just giant bags of chips in huge containers. And you can also do dessert bowls. Chocolate-covered almonds, chocolate-covered popcorn. Pills in bowls! Pot in bowls! Cigarettes in bowls! Condoms in bowls! Whatever floats your bowl!

Bowls are just fucking cool. If I walk into another girl's apartment and it's covered in bowls, I'll immediately think she's hip and get jealous, and that is the highest compliment I can give to any container, or girl.

JUST PUT IT IN A BOWL

THINGS TO PUT IN BOWLS

Nuts (any kind)

Pumpkin seeds

Cherry tomatoes

Baby mozzarella balls (bocconcini), drizzled with olive oil and a sprinkle of salt

Antidepressants

Grapes

Figs (fresh or dried)

Apricots (fresh or dried)

Gumdrops

Jelly beans

Chocolate truffles

Uppers

M&M's

Nonpareils

Pretzels

Mini marshmallows

Tortilla chips

Downers

Hummus

Baby carrots

Guests' cell phones (so people have to talk to one another at your parties)

Olives (set out an extra miniature bowl for the pits)

Raisins

Morning-after pills

Baby bell peppers

Marinated mushrooms

Pita chips

Guacamole

Potato chips

Sunflower seeds (in the shell or out)

And anything you can think of. When in doubt, just put it in a bowl.

BFF BUFFET

MPB

Heyyyyyyyyyyyyyyyyyy Ladiessssssssssssss,

I am so excited to see all of you for Lucy's bachelorette weekend. I've planned everything! And it's going to be literally the best time you've ever had in your entire life. Like, if you suffer from depression, it's going to be cured this weekend with all the fun stuff I have planned. Honestly, I've done soooooo much work for this. You guys have to do literally nothing! NOTHING. All you need to do is bring yourselves, your livers, and also a bunch of other stuff that I'll need you to bring. Please see below.

Please send me your sizes for the T-shirts by EOD. They NEED to be printed TODAY.

Please let me know if you have ANY food allergies. Don't want anyone getting sick on Lucy's special day.

I'll need someone to look for locations, and book one. (Oops, I forgot.)

I'll need another person to organize transportation. It must be a double hexagon HD 4.0 flat-screen-equipped Hummer limo with a detachable rooftop. There are eight in the world, but only the best for our girl. (If you guys really care, this won't be hard.)

Please let me know if you have any problem body parts so I'll know what I'm dealing with in terms of Photoshopping before I upload these photos to Instagram.

Please Venmo me $100,000 by EOD today to pay for the stripper. I know what you're thinking: WTF, right? What a steal! The stripper is actually my assistant Jonathan, so he's doing it at half price, because he loves me. You're welcome.

This is just for Deborah—we don't really know you, because you're Lucy's only friend from summer camp who's coming to this party—can you please write a five-paragraph essay explaining "your deal"? We just want to know what kind of jokes it's cool to make in front of you. Like, what traumas have you experienced in your life? Thanks, girl!

I sort of have impulse-control issues, so I'll need each of you to sign the attached nondisclosure agreement. It just says that if I do anything crazy, like kill someone, you won't tell anyone! All in the name of bachelorette fun.

I will need someone to be my slave because I'm doing so much work.

I need someone to promise they will sleep with Jonathan. His girlfriend just broke up with him and he's having a rough time and he only agreed to do this when I told him he'd get guaranteed sex. He's assured me his heartbreak will NOT affect his stripping.

I'm worried I won't be able to have children (never had it checked out, but just sort of scared), so I'll need someone to sign over their firstborn child.

I'll need everyone to have the time of their lives.

That's about it, guys! Thanks so much. See you soon. Please let me know if you have any problems. Actually, let whoever volunteers to be my slave know!

Love you all,

Penny

. . .

When you get this email, do you scream? Do you run away in fear and decide to say good-bye to all your friends forever? Gabi and I bonded over how much we hated these emails, and she has developed the perfect way to act upon receiving them.

Respond right away, and offer instead to host a special girls' brunch. You will go to the party, but you will not be involved in the planning. You're doing your own thing. You cannot get involved with this Penny girl. You're too busy and important for this email chain. Unsubscribe and just ask for final details. Sure, they'll talk shit about you on that chain, but it's worth it. It's really very worth it.

This is also a kind way to bow out of the weekend if you're not in the mood to crazy drink, don't feel like / can't spend the money on the weekend, or if you just have terrible social anxiety.

Directions follow.

. . .

So first, you need to buy (or ask other people to buy) the following:

- Sparkling wine and orange juice for mimosas: figure 1 bottle of champers for every 4 to 5 people (increase if your guests are heavy drinkers)
- Sparkling water or lemonade: usually 4 to 5 large bottles is good for a 20-person party
- Paper plates, cups, napkins, forks, and serving ware (unless you have enough regular stuff and don't mind doing the dishes / coercing someone else to do so)
- A fruit platter: either make it with various fresh fruits or buy a premade one at the deli)
- A few cheeses and crackers
- A few nice loaves of bread or rolls to serve with the meal

. . .

Here's what to cook:

FRITTATA

This frittata is perfect for these sorts of ridiculous events because (a) pretty much everyone likes eggs; (b) it's low carb, gluten free, and vegetarian, so most guests' dietary restrictions are accommodated; (c) it's as easy as throwing some stuff in a pan and sticking it in the oven. Make one frittata for every 6 to 8 people. Feel free to experiment with fillings.

INGREDIENTS

12 eggs

¾ cup milk or half-and-half (I usually use half-and-half since I'm buying it for people to use in their coffee anyway)

½ teaspoon salt

½ teaspoon pepper

1 (12-ounce) jar roasted red peppers, drained and chopped

1 (10-ounce) package frozen spinach, thawed

6 ounces crumbled goat cheese (feta also works)

DIRECTIONS

- Preheat the oven to 350°F.

- Lightly grease an 11 x 13-inch casserole pan.

- In a large mixing bowl, whisk together the eggs, milk or half-and-half, salt, and pepper.

- Add in the roasted red peppers, spinach, and goat cheese. Stir gently to combine.

- Pour the mixture into the prepared casserole pan.

- Bake for 25 to 30 minutes, or until the eggs are firm.

SERVES 6 TO 8

STRAWBERRY SPINACH SALAD

This pretty salad features a gorgeous medley of sweet, tart, and crunchy, pulled together with a lightly citrusy poppy seed dressing. It makes a fine meal on its own if you're trying to keep things light. You could also top it with some freshly grilled salmon, shrimp, or chicken, if everyone coming to the party is on board with that type of thing.

INGREDIENTS

¼ cup rice vinegar

¼ cup extra-virgin olive oil

Juice of 1 lemon

3 tablespoons poppy seeds

3 tablespoons sugar or honey

Salt and pepper

8 cups packed baby spinach

2 pints fresh strawberries, rinsed, hulled, and sliced

8 ounces crumbled feta cheese

¼ red onion, sliced very thin

2 tablespoons shelled sunflower seeds

DIRECTIONS

• Whisk together the rice vinegar, olive oil, lemon juice, poppy seeds, and sugar or honey. Season with salt and pepper to taste and refrigerate until ready to dress salad.

• To assemble the salad, combine the spinach, strawberries, feta, and onion in a serving bowl.

• Toss well with the dressing and serve, garnished with the sunflower seeds and more pepper to taste.

SERVES 8 TO 10

SUPER SIMPLE CINNAMON ROLLS

These cinnamon rolls accomplish three important things when you're trying to throw a festive brunch: (1) Everyone loves them and is thrilled to eat them. If you have a guest who "just doesn't like cinnamon rolls," ask them to leave. I'm serious. (2) They can be prepped the night before and left to rise in the fridge overnight. In the morning, all you have to do is stick them in the oven and let them fragrance your house with the glorious scent of butter and cinnamon. (3) They are fucking impressive looking and nobody has to know you made them from store-bought dough.

INGREDIENTS

1 stick unsalted butter (½ cup), at room temperature, divided (retain the wrapper)

⅔ cup granulated sugar

1½ tablespoons ground cinnamon

Flour for rolling

1 pound store-bought pizza dough

3 ounces cream cheese, at room temperature

⅔ cup powdered sugar

Vanilla extract

DIRECTIONS

- Use the butter wrapper to grease an 11 × 13-inch baking dish and set aside.

- In a small mixing bowl, stir together 6 tablespoons of the butter, the granulated sugar, and the cinnamon until a smooth paste forms. Set aside.

- On a floured surface, roll the dough out into a rectangle that is approximately 10 × 8 inches.

- Use a rubber scraper to spread the butter-sugar mixture all over the surface of the rectangle.

- Pinching as you go, roll the dough up tightly into a 10-inch cylinder.

- Use a sharp knife to cut the cylinder into ten 1-inch-thick slices and arrange them in the prepared baking dish.

- Cover the dish tightly with plastic wrap and let the dough rise in a warm spot for 1 hour. Alternately, let rise in the refrigerator for at least 8 hours (or overnight).

- Preheat the oven to 350°F.

- Bake the cinnamon rolls for 16 to 18 minutes, or until golden brown.

- While the cinnamon rolls bake, whisk together the remaining 2 tablespoons of butter, the cream cheese, the powdered sugar, and a few drops of vanilla extract until smooth and creamy. If the mixture is too thick, add a few drops of warm water to thin it out slightly.

- Just before serving, spoon the cream cheese glaze over the warm cinnamon rolls.

SERVES 8 TO 10

LEMON-COCONUT DREAM CAKE WITH CREAM CHEESE FROSTING

This cake is so impressive, and so unique, yet insanely easy to make. Even if you haven't made a layer cake before, this one will come out perfectly, we promise. This is mostly thanks to the fact that the whole thing is covered with flaked coconut, which means that any imperfections in your frosting job can be concealed with beautiful, fluffy coconut. Think of it as like Spanx for your cake. Amazing.

INGREDIENTS

For the cakes

2 boxes lemon-flavored cake mix

6 eggs

⅔ cup vegetable, grapeseed, or coconut oil

Juice and zest of 1 lemon

For the Cream Cheese Frosting

1 stick unsalted butter (½ cup), at room temperature

1 (8-ounce) package cream cheese, at room temperature

2 teaspoons vanilla extract

4 cups powdered sugar

For topping the cake

3 cups sweetened, flaked coconut

2 lemons, sliced thinly

NOTE: Feel free to use store-bought vanilla or cream cheese frosting in place of the homemade frosting. You'll need 3 (12-ounce) cans.

For the filling

⅔ cup store-bought lemon curd

DIRECTIONS

Make the cakes

- Preheat the oven to 350°F.

- Grease three 8-inch cake tins, or line them with parchment paper.

- Whisk the cake mix together with the eggs, oil, lemon juice and zest, and 2 cups of water until all lumps have been eliminated.

- Divide the batter between the 3 prepared tins. Bake for approximately 30 minutes, or until the cake springs back when touched with your finger.

- Let the cakes cool completely.

Make the Cream Cheese Frosting

- Beat the butter and cream cheese together in a mixing bowl with an electric beater, in a stand mixer, or in a food processor. Add the vanilla, then beat in the powdered sugar a little at a time until a creamy icing forms.

Assemble the cake

- Place one cake layer on a cake stand or plate, then generously spread about half of the lemon curd over the top. Add the next layer

of cake and follow with the rest of the lemon curd. Place the third cake on top.

• Frost the top and sides of the cake with the frosting. (Don't worry if it's not perfect, the coconut will conceal any lumps or weird-looking spots.)

• Gently press the flaked coconut all over the iced cake.

• Top with a few thin lemon slices and serve.

SERVES 10 TO 12

CHILL GIRL SPORTS SPREAD

GLM

My husband is such a liar.

I mean, his particular brand of lying is relatively innocuous, but still.

"I feel your pain," my mother says to me when I tell her about his wrongdoing. "Your father did the same thing to me."

What I'm talking about here is sports. Specifically the fact that when we met, he claimed to not follow them. A fact that, until learning the truth, I was pretty thrilled about.

And look, I had good reason to believe him. He once texted me after a pickup game of softball that he had "scored so many points!" Points. He called them points.

"It always starts this way," my mom says. "When your father and I were first dating, he would read me Shakespeare love sonnets over the phone and declare that sports were silly. But soon enough, there he was, yelling at the television on Sunday afternoons."

I always knew Evan loved his home state, Wisconsin, and therefore had affection for teams from Wisconsin (the Packers and the Badgers), but until recently, I didn't know that he actually pays attention to the details of the current rosters and understands football strategy. I didn't know that, like my father, he has the capacity to yell at the television. That was his dirty little secret.

"It's not football! It's the Packers!" he insists.

"Do the Packers play football?"

"Well, yes."

"So, we're still talking about football."

But when you love someone, you must find a way to accept them, flaws, lies, well-disguised differences, and all. That is why, since we got together, I have found myself in more than one Packers bar (they are in nearly every city, it turns out), and that is why I hugged him as he cried real tears during "the Pack's" tragic loss to the Seahawks during the playoffs in 2015. And it's also why, for every Super Bowl, I rustle up my sports-lovin' man and his sports-lovin' friends (who probably also duped their partners like Evan did me) a special Super Bowl snack spread.

But, as with every other party in this book, I never do it all myself.

First, I tell everyone to bring beer. That's the most appropriate thing to drink while you watch sports, right? I think? All I know is that it would really suck to run out of it (and in my experience, when sports lovers are engaged in sports watching, they're usually unwilling to get off the couch and reup the brewskis). And ask one or two people to grab a few fun nonalcoholic drinks; it's always good to have alternatives.

Also pick up or instruct peeps to bring a few fun crunchy snacks like popcorn, tortilla chips, and nuts.

Now here's your menu, whether you are a Sporty Sally or, like me, more of an Acquiescing Anna:

BAKED SRIRACHA HOT WINGS

Baking chicken wings is much easier than (and in my opinion, just as good as) frying them. I often double or triple this recipe if our crowd is going to be big.

INGREDIENTS

2 sticks unsalted butter (1 cup)

1 cup sriracha

1 teaspoon salt

5 pounds party wings

3 ribs celery, cut into sticks

3 carrots, peeled and cut into sticks

Ranch or blue cheese dressing

DIRECTIONS

- Melt the butter in a saucepan over low heat. Add the sriracha and salt, whisking well to combine. Remove from heat and let the sauce cool.

- Divide the wings between two 1-gallon-size zip-top bags. Add one-quarter of the sauce to each bag, and reserve the remaining half of the sauce. Push as much air out of the bags as possible and move the wings around in the bags to ensure they are well coated. Marinate in the refrigerator for at least an hour, or as long as overnight.

- Preheat the oven to 425°F.

- Line 2 baking sheets with foil, lightly grease them with oil or cooking spray, and set aside.

- Remove the wings from the bags and shake off any excess marinade from each one. Discard the marinade.

- Arrange the wing pieces skin-side up on the prepared baking sheets, making sure to leave a little room between pieces.

- Bake undisturbed for 30 to 35 minutes, until the wings are golden brown and release easily from the baking sheet. Using a pair of tongs or a spatula, turn the pieces over and return to the oven to bake for an additional 15 to 20 minutes, until very crisp.

- When the wings have finished cooking, remove from the oven.

- Transfer the reserved sauce to a baking dish or mixing bowl.

- Working in batches, toss the cooked wings in the sauce until well coated, then transfer them to a serving platter.

- Serve the wings immediately, with the celery, carrots, and ranch or blue cheese dressing for dipping.

SERVES 6 TO 8

CHIPOTLE-MAPLE PULLED PORK

Serve this pulled pork with Hawaiian rolls or adorable slider/mini hamburger rolls and let people make their own little sandwiches.

INGREDIENTS

2 tablespoons extra-virgin olive oil or vegetable oil

1 medium onion, sliced

4 cloves garlic, minced

5 pounds pork stew meat (cubed pork shoulder)

1 (32-ounce) can diced tomatoes, with their juice

2 chipotle peppers (from a can, packed in adobo sauce), chopped

4 cups chicken, beef, or vegetable stock

⅓ cup maple syrup (preferably Grade B dark amber)

¼ cup brown sugar

Ground black pepper

NOTE: You can also make this recipe with beef brisket instead of pork—a great option if you have kosher or halal guests. It also works well with chicken thighs.

DIRECTIONS

• Heat the oil in a large soup pot (make sure it has a fitted lid) or Dutch oven over medium heat. Add the onion and garlic and cook until fragrant, about 2 minutes.

• Add the pork to the pot and brown, about 1 minute on each side.

• Add the diced tomatoes, chipotles, and stock. Stir well to combine.

• Gently stir in the maple syrup, brown sugar, and a few grinds of black pepper.

• Cover the pot and cook for 60 to 90 minutes, until the liquid has been reduced to a thick sauce and the meat is very tender.

• Remove from heat.

• Remove the meat and put it on a large, preferably rimmed cutting board. Use 2 forks to pull pork into shreds.

• Return the pulled pork to the sauce and stir well to combine.

• Serve pulled pork on sandwich buns with coleslaw, or on its own.

SERVES 6 TO 8

LEGIT ONION DIP

You are too good for onion dip from a mix. Besides, the real stuff (which is SO much better) is as easy as sautéing some onions and mixing them with a few other things. This is a good one to make in advance, because sitting in the fridge for a day or two will make it even tastier.

INGREDIENTS

2 tablespoons extra-virgin olive oil or vegetable oil

1 large or 2 medium yellow onions, diced

¼ teaspoon salt

1½ cups sour cream or Greek yogurt

¾ cup mayonnaise (preferably full-fat—come on, just do it)

½ teaspoon pepper

¼ teaspoon garlic powder

DIRECTIONS

• Heat the oil in a large frying pan over medium-low heat.

• Add the onions and salt. Stir well.

• Cook the onions until they are very brown, about 20 minutes. Don't stir them again, but do check periodically to make sure they're not burning. If they start to burn, turn down the heat.

• Remove from heat and set aside to cool.

• Stir the rest of the ingredients together in a mixing bowl, and then add the cooled onions. Stir gently to combine.

• Refrigerate until completely chilled, then stir well before serving.

SERVES 8 TO 10

FUDGY AS FUCK BROWNIES

These rich, chewy brownies are the perfect finish to your sporty spread. Feel free to really push the sports theme by serving them with "balls" of ice cream. Get it? Balls?

INGREDIENTS

1½ sticks unsalted butter (¾ cup)

8 ounces semisweet chocolate chips

1 cup unsweetened cocoa powder

2 cups granulated sugar

2 eggs

1 teaspoon vanilla extract

1 cup all-purpose flour

½ teaspoon salt

DIRECTIONS

• Preheat the oven to 350°F.

• Lightly grease a 9 × 13-inch baking pan.

• Fill a small saucepan with tap water to a depth of about 2 inches. Cover the saucepan with a heatproof bowl to create a double boiler. Turn the heat up to high and melt the butter and chocolate chips in the bowl, whisking frequently. Carefully remove the bowl from the pot and turn off the heat.

• Transfer the melted chocolate and butter to a mixing bowl and whisk in the cocoa powder, sugar, eggs, vanilla, flour, and salt. Add ½ cup water and whisk until the mixture is very smooth.

• Pour the batter into the prepared pan and bake for 22 to 25 minutes, or until top is shiny and few crumbs cling to an inserted toothpick.

• Cool until the brownies are warm or room temperature. Cut into squares and serve.

SERVES 6 TO 8

CLAIM TO FLAME: HOW TO PULL OFF A PERFECT SUMMER BBQ

GLM

First of all, barbecuing and grilling are not identical:

BARBECUED: Food slow-cooked over low heat using smoke from natural wood. *Barbecue* can be used as a noun, verb, or adjective. It is a destination, a meal, a sandwich, a party, a cooking technique, and a descriptor for almost anything cooked outdoors, charred, or smoky.

GRILLED: Food cooked over high heat for a short period of time to sear the outside and quickly cook the inside. Grill roasting over indirect heat falls somewhere between classic grilling and barbecue.

If you are lucky enough to have a grill, take full advantage of it by throwing outdoor BBQ shindigs as often as possible. Don't own one? See if a generous friend will share one with you, or consider buying a small Weber one (Evan and I call ours Grilligan, and he lives on his own little island, AKA our tiny balcony). You can cook large amounts on its small surface if you work in batches, and it's easy to transport if you travel (or move!).

Whenever I grill, I ask my pals to bring over beer, and I make a big batch of Bad Bitch Margaritas (see page 205) or When in Doubt, Make Sangria (see page 192). I provide the buns, condiments, chips, and a few basic proteins and vegetables (burgers, chicken thighs or breasts, vegetarian sausages, and portobello mushrooms are my go-tos).

Once you have your ingredients assembled, it's just a matter of cooking. Here's how to make your grilling safe and easy.

Prepare and Heat Your Grill

Heat the grill (charcoal or gas) for 20 minutes, or until it reaches 500-plus degrees, to sterilize it and prepare for searing food.

NOTE: If you're using charcoal, the coals are ready when they turn white and achieve a red glow. Look for charcoal on sale during the winter months to save a few dollars.

Determine Your Cooking Method: Direct or Indirect

Use the direct method to cook foods quickly: simply place your protein on the grate directly over the heat source. This method works well for chicken breasts, steaks, and seafood.

Consider the indirect method for foods that require longer than 20 minutes to cook, such as whole chickens, boneless turkey roasts, and pork ribs. If you're using charcoal, spread the briquettes around the edges of the grill and place the protein in the center with a drip tray underneath.

Prepare Your Food

Always use one set of tongs for raw food and another for cooked food. Mark the tongs to avoid cross-contamination (or, like me, use a blue-handled set for raw food and a red-handled one for cooked).

Always discard used marinade once meat is placed on the grill. It's not safe to ingest.

Lightly oil the food or the grill before cooking. You can use cooking spray or olive oil and a brush to do this.

If you want to get really fancy, use hickory, alder, or mesquite wood chips to add extra flavor to your cooking. Soak the chips in water for one hour, then add them directly to the charcoal or place them in a smoker box on the grate in your gas grill. Adding chips to your grill is less expensive (and more likely to be okay with your landlord) than building a wood fire.

A meat thermometer is a great way to check whether your food is done without cutting into it. Remove the meat when it's about 5 degrees below the desired serving temperature (approximately 5 minutes before it's done), and then cover it tightly with foil and allow it to rest for 5 to 10 minutes. The meat will continue to cook during this time, so it will be perfect when you're ready to serve it.

Once the food is cooked, platter it up, set it out, and let the hungry masses eat. Oh, and don't forget to turn your grill off (or put out the fire) when you finish cooking. Once you've had two or three glasses of sangria, it can be easy to forget, so do it before you get tipsy.

YOUR FIRST THANKSGIVING

GLM

At last, we have come to the biggest and most stressful night of entertaining: Thanksgiving. You are doing it. You are hosting your first Thanksgiving. Congratulations, and take twenty-seven deep breaths. Everything is going to be fine and awesome and great. Buy yourself a present when you're done. (Better yet, have your guests get you presents. Maybe you should register for Thanksgiving? Just an idea . . .)

So perhaps you're living far away from where you grew up and you want to have a little taste of home. Maybe you're planning a Friendsgiving and have been put in charge of most of the cooking. Or maybe the Thanksgiving turkey torch has finally been passed from your great-aunt Eunice to you, and on Thursday all the members of your extended family will descend upon your dining table.

Do not panic.

Hosting a Thanksgiving meal is involved, but it doesn't have to be hard. Organization and a little thoughtful planning are the keys to making your prep go smoothly and your meal go off with as few hitches as possible.

The first thing you have to know is that there is one trick that will make your Thanksgiving vastly less stressful and much more enjoyable: *don't cook everything*. Yup, you read that right. Remember your mom on Thanksgivings past, rushing around the kitchen, freaking out about timing the baking of six pies and four kinds of potatoes and the turkey (plus a Tofurkey for your vegetarian brother and his rotating selection of hippie girlfriends)? Learn from her mistakes and keep it simple. This is how.

The first step is to reach out to your most responsible / culinarily gifted guests and ask that they bring:

- Two or three appetizers (a cheese or two and crackers, vegetables and dip, meatballs on toothpicks, bacon-wrapped dates, etc.)
- Two or three vegetarian sides, which will do the additional job of serving as the main meal for any vegetarian or turkey-loathing guests at your table (green beans, sweet potatoes, mashed potatoes, mac and cheese, creamed onions, etc.)
- A few desserts (pumpkin pie, apple pie, pecan pie, ice cream, etc.)

Next, you'll need to go shopping. Because it's going to be a lot of stuff, consider dividing this up into a few trips or using grocery delivery services, if you have those in your area. Go through the following recipes and lists, and buy (or ask someone to pick up) everything you don't already have on hand.

Here's what you'll need:

BEVERAGES

(Guests worth their salt will likely bring beverages to share—feel free to send them specific requests according to this list to save yourself further shopping trips.)

- Champagne, prosecco, or other sparkling white wine (Champagne is typically more expensive). Serve this to start; one bottle for every four people.

- If you have any nondrinkers, get sparkling apple cider or sparkling lemonade for them.

- Pinot noir (which goes well with turkey). One bottle for every two people.

TURKEY

INGREDIENTS

1 thawed turkey (1 pound per person—this includes bone weight. Obviously, subtract vegetarians). If you are expecting a small group (fewer than 6), consider cooking a turkey breast or, better yet, 1 or 2 whole chickens.

Salt and pepper

1 cup melted unsalted butter or extra-virgin olive oil, divided

2 cups chicken broth, turkey broth, or white wine

DIRECTIONS

- Position an oven rack in the bottom third of your oven and preheat the oven to 450°F.

- Rub the turkey all over with salt and pepper and arrange it breast-up in a large roasting pan. (Don't worry about trussing or stuffing the turkey.)

- Rub the turkey all over with ½ cup of the butter or oil.

- Pour the broth or wine into the bottom of the roasting pan.

- Put the turkey in the oven, on the lowest rack, and immediately turn the heat down to 350°F.

- Roast the turkey for 13 minutes per pound, basting every 45 minutes. (This just means brushing the turkey all over with the liquid from the bottom of the pan. You can use a turkey baster, a pastry brush, or even a small ladle.)

- During the last 45 minutes of roasting, baste the turkey 2 to 3 times with the remaining ½ cup butter or oil. (This will help turn the skin really golden brown and crispy.)

- Check the turkey for doneness by inserting a thermometer into the breast. It should read 160°F. Let the cooked turkey rest for at least 20 minutes before carving it (this will bring the temperature up to 165°F, which is the temperature you should serve it at).

- Save the drippings—you'll use them to make gravy later.

To carve the turkey

- Get a sharp carving knife and a large carving fork (or a large table fork).

- Place the turkey on a carving board with lipped edges to catch the juices.

- Beginning halfway up the breast, slice straight down, perpendicular to the turkey's spine.

- Continue to slice breast meat, starting your cut at a higher point each time. Repeat until the whole breast is sliced.

- Transfer the slices to a serving platter.

- Hold the end of a drumstick, place your knife between the drumstick and the body of the turkey, and cut straight through the skin to the joint. If your knife is sharp, it should go straight through. If you have trouble, grab some kitchen scissors and snip it.

- Remove the entire leg by pulling out and back, using the sharp tip of the knife to slice it off the bird. Separate the thigh and drumstick at the joint, so you have two pieces. Add them to the serving platter and repeat with the remaining thigh and drumstick.

- Insert the fork in the wing to steady the turkey, then make a long horizontal cut above the wing joint through the body frame.

- Remove the wing, add it to the serving platter, and repeat with the second wing.

STUFFING

INGREDIENTS

3 tablespoons unsalted butter

1 large onion, diced

1 head celery, diced

1 loaf of white or whole wheat bread, cut into ½-inch cubes

1 bunch fresh parsley, chopped

3 cups low-sodium turkey or chicken broth, divided

1 teaspoon salt

1 teaspoon pepper

DIRECTIONS

- Preheat the oven to 375°F.

- Grease a 9 x 13-inch baking pan.

- In a large skillet, melt the butter over medium heat.

- Add the onion and celery. Cook, stirring occasionally, until the vegetables begin to brown, about 10 minutes.

- Scrape the onion-celery mixture into a large bowl and add the cubed bread and parsley.

- Stir in 2½ cups of the broth and the salt and pepper.

- Pack the stuffing in the prepared baking pan.

- Drizzle with the remaining ½ cup of the broth, cover the pan with aluminum foil, and bake for 25 to 28 minutes.

- Remove the foil and bake for an additional 7 to 8 minutes to crisp the top.

SERVES 8

CRANBERRY SAUCE

This is a standard cranberry sauce, freshened up with a touch of orange. Feel free to use lime, lemon, or even a little chili (chopped fresh ones, or your favorite hot sauce to taste).

INGREDIENTS

1 cup sugar

4 cups fresh or frozen cranberries

Juice and zest of 1 orange

DIRECTIONS

- Combine all the ingredients in a medium pot over medium heat and bring to a boil.

- Reduce heat to medium-low and cook, uncovered, stirring occasionally, for 45 to 50 minutes, until the cranberries completely break down and a jam forms.

SERVES 8 TO 10

GRAVY

Don't bother with gravy helper when it's beyond simple to make it fresh.

INGREDIENTS

4 tablespoons unsalted butter (¼ cup)

¼ cup all-purpose flour

4 cups turkey drippings (the stuff in the bottom of the pan after you cook the turkey)

DIRECTIONS

- Melt the butter in a medium saucepan over medium-high heat. Gradually whisk in the flour and cook, whisking constantly, until the mixture begins to turn light brown.

- Whisk in the turkey drippings, 1 cup at a time.

- Bring to a boil, then reduce to a simmer and cook, whisking frequently, until the gravy is thick and creamy, about 10 minutes.

- Remove from heat and taste for seasoning, adding salt and pepper if the gravy needs it. (It likely won't, as the drippings are already pretty salty, but it's good to check.)

SERVES 8 TO 10

Other Things to Buy

- Dinner rolls (figure 2 per person—you'll have leftovers, but they're good for turkey sandwiches the next day)
- Salted butter for the rolls
- Coffee, tea, or a digestif to serve with dessert (you can also ask guests to bring this)
- Aluminum baking trays or roasting pans, if needed (helpful if you don't own all the necessary pans)
- A meat thermometer. It will take all the guesswork out of turkey cooking. They're relatively cheap and are generally available at regular grocery stores.

What to Do Thanksgiving Day

1. First, roast the turkey. You'll want to start this early in the day. The general rule for cooking turkeys is 13 minutes per pound, so if you are cooking a 20-pound bird, plan for a little over 4 hours of roasting. You'll want to have the turkey out of the oven about an hour before your guests arrive (so it can rest and so the oven can be made available for other items that need to be warmed up).

2. While the turkey is roasting, make the cranberry sauce and prep the stuffing for the oven. Keep the cranberry sauce in its pot on the stovetop and pack the stuffing into a baking dish (or two, depending on how much you are making).

Whew! Now for the Homestretch!

3. When the turkey is finished, let it rest on a carving board for at least 20 minutes before you carve into it. Use this time to bake the stuffing.

4. At this point, your guests are likely showing up. Have them set out their appetizers and stick any side dishes they brought that need to be warmed up, along with the rolls (on an ungreased baking sheet), into the oven with the stuffing until everything is nice and hot, about 20 minutes. Transfer the hot rolls into a basket lined with a clean dish towel or napkin.

5. Just before you carve the turkey, make the gravy and transfer it to a bowl with a spoon, or a gravy boat (whoa, you have a gravy boat?).

6. Ask everyone to help you bring the food to the table, and invite your guests to be seated.

7. Finally, raise a glass, toast yourself, your friends, and the joys of pulling off the cooking of an enormous meal, and dig in.

8. Make everyone else do the dishes. Obviously.

CHAPTER 6

Let's Get Drunk

A night of heavy drinking can lead to an onslaught of awful next-morning memories. Such as:

1. You drunk texted someone, "u up?"

2. They responded, "Cum ova," and you went.

3. They ignored you and you are embarrassed.

4. You slept with someone you shouldn't have slept with.

5. You did other stuff with someone you shouldn't have done other stuff with.

6. You begged your best friend, a gay guy, to make out with you.

7. You left an angry voicemail. You left any voicemail at all.

8. You locked yourself out of your house and slept on your stoop.

9. You lost the entire contents of your purse.

10. You told everyone blatant lies all night. You swear they felt like truths in the moment. (Example: "The Dalai Lama fell in love with me once." Translation: I read a Wikipedia article on his best quotes.)

11. You spent a million dollars on Ubers.

12. You broke your whole home.

13. You ate everything.

14. You ruined your shoes.

15. You lost your shoes.

16. Someone threw your shoes out the window. (Hey, get in control of your shoes. What's wrong with you?)

17. You spilled all your secrets.

18. You spilled all of someone else's secrets.

19. Those secrets were really secret and spilling them is going to get you fired.

20. You're just, like, deeply ashamed, on a cosmic level.

Want to know the number one way to avoid this sort of insanity? Easy: Drink at home. Invite people over to join you if you want (hey, put some snacks out too, if you want!). But whatever you do, bring the party to you. You'll have a much quicker trip to the bathroom should you go overboard!

Because we can't guarantee that you won't drink too many Manhattans in Heels (page 193) or Dirty Girl Martinis (page 198) and try to make out with your ex, or drunk-dial your boss, or scream-sing all of Taylor Swift's first and second albums between sips of When in Doubt, Make Sangria (page 192) on your balcony until your neighbors call the cops, but at least when you do it, you'll be within fifty feet of your bed (significantly less, if you live in New York). So use this chapter to drink at home. You (and your going-out shoes) will thank us. —GLM & MPB

FORMULA IS FOR BABIES . . . AND COCKTAILS: THE BASIC COCKTAIL

GLM

Hosting parties on a budget can be quite a challenge. And when it comes time to stock the bar, it's always the same problem at the store: what to buy, how much to buy, and what can you make with it that everyone will like? Most people will get the basics: a handle of vodka, a handle of rum, and perhaps whiskey or bourbon. Some OJ, cranberry, Coke, Diet Coke, Sprite, tonic, etc. Oh, and don't forget the limes, maybe lemons, napkins, cups, ice—and the list goes on. While you've offered your guests a respectable basic bar to mix their own drinks, you've also spent quite a lot of money.

As the food and drink person in my circle of friends, I've noticed that when I go to parties with this kind of bar setup, I'm often asked if I can "make something good" for someone. It becomes my task to check out the ingredients at the bar (or what's left of them) and improvise "something good." The next thing I know, I'm making this concoction for a bunch of people who are happy to drink anything that they didn't have to put much thought into. One night at a party, while mixing up random cocktail after random cocktail, per my friends' requests, I decided to put this phenomenon to good use. In the process, I accidentally figured out a way to spend half as much on my "bar" and serve a special drink that makes a lasting impact.

The next time I went shopping for alcohol to stock a party, I decided to skip the part where people make their own drinks and go right to the part where I'm making them. So I made two cocktails. Two really big cocktails. I came up with two different drinks that I could make in pitchers. I then set up my bar with a bowl of ice, glasses, napkins, and my two pitchers, which I simply refilled as the night went on. It was a simple and very cost-effective way to host a party and leave a nice impression on my guests.

The trick is to use pretty much the same spirits but with different mixers so that there is variety. I recommend vodka as the main liquor, but you could easily substitute rum. Either way, use plain, clear, unflavored spirits. I recommend Seagram's vodka or Castillo Silver rum—both are good quality yet relatively cheap.

Triple sec should be a staple of any home bar. It's like a good bottle of hot sauce: it stays good for ages, a little goes a long way, and you can mix it with just about anything. A one-liter bottle costs around $15 and will last through many parties.

It's time to let you in on a little bartending secret. Don't get too excited, I have no idea how maraschino cherries get so red either—just a drink-making formula that you can adapt to almost any cocktail.

It's called the 2-1-3:

- 2 parts primary liquor: for now, primary liquors will be vodka or rum
- 1 part cordial or liqueur; which will refer to triple sec, peach schnapps, raspberry liqueur, or other flavored cordials
- 3 parts juice or mix, although a little more to fill the glass is okay

Measure in ounces for individual cocktails, or in cups for making pitchers and bowls. Just stick to the 2-1-3 ratio. Remember that individual cocktails should be made in a glass full of ice, while large drinks made in pitchers or carafes should be kept separate from ice until ready for service. In either case, a little stir and you're good to go. No garnish needed.

I figured I'd start you off with some basic everyday drink recipes, but feel free to experiment. Just stick to the formula and see what you can come up with. Now let's make some drinks! Here's a handy cheat sheet for some classics:

- **SEX ON THE BEACH:** vodka, peach schnapps, cranberry juice and orange juice[*]

- **WOO-WOO:** vodka, peach schnapps, cranberry juice

- **PEARL HARBOR:** vodka, melon liqueur, pineapple juice

- **MELON BALL:** vodka, melon liqueur, orange juice

- **PURPLE HOOTER:** vodka, raspberry liqueur or raspberry schnapps, cranberry juice

- **RUMRITA:** rum, triple sec, sweet-and-sour mix

- **TROPICAL BREEZE:** rum, amaretto, pineapple juice and orange juice

- **CARIBBEAN BREEZE:** rum, peach schnapps, cranberry juice and orange juice

- **LOST IN BERMUDA:** rum, melon liqueur, pineapple juice

---

* In the case of multiple juices or mixers, split the amount so that the total makes 3 parts.

HOW TO STOCK YOUR BAR WITHOUT SPENDING ALL YOUR RENT MONEY

GLM

Drinking at home is always fun, but it's so much better when you have everything you need to make great cocktails. Just as you need a few specific tools and gadgets to keep your kitchen running, and some basic pantry items to make up your meals, your home bar needs outfitting. These are the basics for drink mixing and cocktail shaking at home.

Equipment

SHAKER TIN AND STRAINER: Next time you go to a bar, order an apple martini or a cosmo and watch the bartender make it. She'll pour the ingredients into a tin shaker and use it to shake the drink before straining into a glass. Like a knife and cutting board for cooking, a shaker set is the most basic tool for cocktail making. Get yours at a restaurant supply store and you should pay no more than $12. Look for plain stainless steel tins (15-ounce and 30-ounce) and a strainer. For a few bucks more you can opt for the all-in-one set that includes a fitted cover with a built-in strainer. You can find these at Target, BevMo!, or on ye olde internet.

While you're at it, pick up a muddler and, if you don't already have one, a wine bottle opener.

CITRUS JUICERS: Juicers are the quickest way to make fresh orange, lemon, lime, or grapefruit juice, and they look so cute! Plus, you can juice the citrus right into the jigger to measure.

GLASSWARE: We like using mason jars (we know, so Brooklyn), but IKEA, Target, and thrift shops are great places to get whole sets on the cheap (or buy individual pieces, for a more eclectic look).

LIQUOR: The following list is based on the principle of buying few but versatile products. It's really the only way to save money and still have a lot to offer.

VODKA AND RUM: The building blocks to so many cocktails, and the most versatile and useful spirits to have around. If you're a gin drinker, add that as well.

WHISKEY: Bourbon, rye, scotch—whatever you like and enjoy drinking. I like to buy an inexpensive one for mixing in cocktails and a higher-quality variety for sipping.

TRIPLE SEC (OR COINTREAU IF YOU'RE FANCY): You'll use this in margaritas, cosmopolitans, and just about every other fruity cocktail.

Garnishes

ICE CUBES: Do you always forget to buy ice when you're entertaining? Do you end up last-minute frantically texting your friends like, "Somebody please pick up ice or else the world will explode right now," and then everyone's on their way and you have no ice, and you feel all your efforts have gone to waste because the one most basic element is missing? Well, we do. And a perfect way to ensure this doesn't happen is to make ice cubes a part of your garnish. We love edible flower petals, pomegranate seeds, fresh herbs (think mint and rosemary), berries, and cucumbers, but anything from lemon slices to gummy bears to mood stabilizers will do. These cubes flavor your beverage as they melt, and they make you look like you were born in Pinterest-city.

CHERRIES: We love garnishing cocktails with good old-fashioned maraschino cherries, as well as showcasing our tongue dexterity by attempting to tie their stems into knots. We always keep a pre-tied stem hidden under our tongues because neither of us has ever succeeded in doing it in our mouths (nor, we assume, has anyone ever in the history of time). Anyhow, darker, more serious cherries, like Luxardos or Morellos, are a fab bar staple to keep on hand.

RASPBERRIES ON ROSEMARY: We realize that a full stick of rosemary in a beverage might seem a little unorthodox, but trust us. It's especially good with gin-based drinks (the herb plays up gin's juniper berry flavor), as well as anything citrusy or fizzy. Make sure to drop these in your cocktails with the raspberries on the bottom so they'll add fruity sweetness.

GARNISH FOR SLUTTY/VIRGIN MARY: Sure, you can jam all your savory garnishes directly into the Mary itself, *or* you can layer them elegantly onto a long skewer and stick it directly into the drink, making it that much easier and more fun to snack as you sip.

TOASTED MARSHMALLOWS ON A STICK: Marshmallows are good, but everyone knows toasted (let's be honest: slightly burnt) 'mallows are where it's at. We take the campfire indoors by poking as many as we can onto a toothpick and lighting them on fire for a few seconds (trust us, that's plenty of time to char them nicely) and dunking them in our hot cocoa, with or without booze added. Just remember: if you *are* adding booze, blow out the fire before you add them to your drink so as to avoid singeing off your eyebrows.

HOW TO MAKE CHEAP WINE TASTE EXPENSIVE (OR AT LEAST MODERATELY PRICED)

GLM

Snobs be damned, cheap wine is fabulous. We're not talking about cooking wine or sticky-sweet varieties (ask me about the time in high school when I drank an entire bottle of Manischewitz at a party and got purple puke all over the front lawn). I mean the $3 to $6 bottles you always end up sticking in your grocery basket, figuring they're not good enough for company, so you sip them alone. Well, with a few little tricks, your $3 wine can taste like a $50 bottle of wine. Or at least one in the low- to midtwenties range.

DECANT IT. This simply means transfer it to a new container—like a pitcher or another bottle. The act of transferring and moving the wine around helps to introduce oxygen into it, which improves the flavor. Note: don't try to decant sparkling wine, as it will only make the wine go flat faster, which improves the flavor only for older, more expensive sparkling wines.

AERATE IT. When decanting isn't enough, try aerating your wine, by either pouring it through a wine aerator (look for them in wine stores and cooking supply shops) or simply stirring it. My favorite way to do this without a wine aerator is to pour the wine into a large jar or pitcher and whisk it with a wire whisk for 30 to 60 seconds. Then let it sit for a few minutes. You will most likely find the wine's flavor to be improved.

CHILL IT. Even if it's red. But no ice cubes.

BLEND IT. This may sound crazy, but I promise you, nobody will ever know. If you mix a bottle of cheap wine with a bottle of slightly less cheap wine in a big pitcher, aerate it well, and put it in front of your friends, do you know what they'll do?

They'll smile because you just put a HUGE pitcher of wine in front of them. Then they'll drink it and comment on how unique it tastes. I promise. Try it.

MULL IT. Simmer your wine with a few cloves, cinnamon sticks, cardamom pods, and orange peels. Not only will your house smell amazing, but your crappy wine will mellow into the ultimate stay-warm sipper.

WHEN IN DOUBT, MAKE SANGRIA

INGREDIENTS

1 orange, rind on, half cut into small chunks, seeds removed; half sliced, for garnish

½ apple, skin on, cored and chopped into small pieces

2–3 tablespoons sugar, or more to taste

6 ounces orange juice, plus more to taste

2½ ounces brandy, plus more to taste

1 (750-milliliter) bottle cheap red wine (white also works)

Ice cubes

DIRECTIONS

- Place the orange chunks, apple, and sugar in a large pitcher and muddle with a muddler or wooden spoon until fruit resembles a thick paste.

- Add the orange juice and brandy and stir well to combine.

- Add the wine and stir, then taste and adjust sugar as needed.

- Add the ice and stir once more to chill. Serve as is, or with more ice. Garnish with orange slices.

SERVES 4 TO 6

MANHATTAN IN HEELS

MPB

Hey, you chic drunks, what's up?

Despite all the things I tell you in this book, I swear I'm a functioning member of society. I've held jobs and responsibilities and people! In fact, people often tell me that I'm an old soul or that I'm clearly from Manhattan because I'm sophisticated. This is my favorite compliment to get. But all that respectability goes completely out the window when I get drunk.

Manhattan in Heels? More like Manhattan in Broken Heels That She Loses Later in the Night, or Maybe Throws out the Window as a Cool Gag. Shocker: I like to steal when I'm drunk. My apartment is currently decorated with some candlesticks from a very well-known Los Angeles nighttime establishment, and I've got a bunch of forks from a curated kitschy place in Silver Lake. (They look great, thanks for asking.) I'm super loud when I'm drunk. I'll make out with just about anyone. I lose everything. Once, I locked myself out of my parents' apartment and slept in the hallway. I went into the stairwell when their doorman brought them their morning *New York Times* because I was so ashamed. None of this is revolutionary. We all do dumb shit when we're drunk, but there comes a point when you've just got to stop, at least in front of certain people.

I've developed a plan for these instances, the times when I want to be sophisticated Miranda and not shoeless Miranda. My strategy for those times is to choose one drink and have only two glasses of it throughout the night. (I know, this is very genius and you've never heard of it before.) I choose the Manhattan, because I like it and it reminds me of the person I'd like to be. You may choose whichever drink you like, but the greatest advice I can give you in my young life is to have only two drinks at a party.

Here's why:

1. You will be yourself. Sure, you're a little lubricated and can have fun conversations, but basically you are you. You can meet people you like and may even want to know in normal postparty life.

2. If someone hot asks to get you a drink, you will only have had two drinks, so another one won't put you over the edge.

3. If you are actually into this hot someone, you can act cool and keep your wits about you. You won't start crying if they don't ask for your number right away.

4. You'll leave at a normal time and won't feel the need to stay late and party for the hell of it.

5. You won't steal.

6. You won't do a stand-up routine about the host's weird art.

7. You won't make up lies that seem like truth in the moment. For example, "Yes, I got a full ride to Harvard, but it just didn't seem like the right school for me."

8. You won't get fully nude and jump into the pool.

9. You won't smoke cigarettes.

10. You will feel fine the next morning.

Now, I've done this plan twice, but I was really happy those two times. So, if you ever run into me at a party, and I've had eighteen drinks, just be cool.

MANHATTAN IN HEELS

INGREDIENTS

2 dashes Angostura bitters

1 ounce sweet vermouth

2½ ounces bourbon

1 maraschino cherry

DIRECTIONS

- Fill a short glass two-thirds full with ice.

- Add the bitters, vermouth, and bourbon.

- Add the cherry and crush it against the side of the glass with a spoon. Stir and serve.

SERVES 1

FRENCH 69

MPB

This is our version of a French 75. We call it a French 69, because 69 is funny and because we're choosing this as our sexy drink.

There are many different reasons to get drunk. You can get drunk because someone hurt your feelings deeply—my favorite reason to get drunk. You can get drunk to celebrate—my favorite reason to get drunk. You can get drunk because you're bored—my favorite reason to get drunk. But my favorite reason to get drunk is to get a little bit flirty. I'm not naturally the most touchy-feely person, but if I have a little something in me, I become the kind of girl who hops up backward onto a kitchen island or pulls a bread crumb out of a guy's beard, or forgets to lock the door while peeing at a party. You know, sexy things like that.

Champagne is flirty and light and usually puts you in a fun mood. So the French 69 is the perfect drink to get things going with that special someone. More important, it's pretty cheap to make and looks impressive. You can mix a whole pitcher of it for not much money. Invite your honey over, either alone or as part of a group. Perhaps one or both of you will be a little shy to make the first move, but by the end of the night you'll be smiley and all over each other.

I make a pitcher of French 69 for every dinner party I have. Three times it has made someone spend the night. Two of those times it was my best friend, Hillary, because she was too drunk to go home, but that's okay. Friendship is important.

INGREDIENTS

For the simple syrup

1 cup granulated sugar

1 cup water

For the cocktail

1 lemon

1½ ounces gin

½ ounce simple syrup

1 cup ice cubes

2 ounces dry sparkling wine, such as brut Champagne, chilled

DIRECTIONS

Make the simple syrup

- Combine the sugar and water in a medium saucepan over medium heat. Stir until the sugar dissolves.

- Increase the heat and bring to a boil, then reduce heat to medium and simmer 3 minutes.

- Transfer the syrup to a bowl and chill thoroughly.

Make the cocktail

- Using a zester or paring knife, slice the peel from the lemon in a long, thin spiral.

- Juice the lemon, and pour ¾ ounce (1½ tablespoons) of the lemon juice into a cocktail shaker.

- Add the gin and simple syrup.

- Add the ice and shake vigorously for 10 seconds.

- Strain into a chilled Champagne flute and top with the sparkling wine.

- Curl the lemon peel around your finger to create a twist at least 6 inches long.

- Garnish the drink with the twist and serve immediately.

SERVES 1

DIRTY GIRL MARTINI

GLM

While I'll drink bourbon straight, and I love a good tequila or mezcal, I haven't come around to vodka yet. Even the good stuff tastes like rubbing alcohol to me. Some better brands of rubbing alcohol than others, but definitely something I would use to clean out a cut.

In college, my friend Jen taught me how to mix Crystal Light with vodka to make fruit-flavored drinks that got us smashed basically without our realizing it. When you're nineteen and have the cheapest vodka and a terrible fake ID you can buy in your dorm, this is maybe in the realm of appropriate. Anytime after that? No longer okay.

That's why adult ladies who want to drink vodka but not really taste it turn to the drink of the eighties, the dirty martini. It's only called dirty because olive brine is added. I realize it sounds like a weird addition, but if you've ever had a pickleback (Google it), you know that punchy, vinegary flavors go well with booze.

Plus, it's so fun to order. Especially if you ask for it "extra dirty" in a husky Scarlett Johansson voice.

INGREDIENTS

Twist of lemon peel

2½ ounces vodka or gin

½ ounce brine from cocktail olive jar

⅛ ounce extra-dry vermouth

1 cup ice cubes

2 cocktail olives, for garnish

DIRECTIONS

- Use a lighter or match to light the tip of the lemon peel twist on fire. Blow out immediately (it shouldn't burn very much). Set aside.

- Shake the vodka or gin, brine, and vermouth with the ice in a cocktail shaker.

- Strain into a chilled martini glass or cocktail glass.

- Garnish with the olives and burnt twist and serve.

SERVES 1

NO FUCKS NEGRONI

GLM & MPB

The No Fucks Negroni Girl is awesome. She walks into a bar wearing a black turtle-neck, sits down by herself in a corner booth, orders her drink, and looks cool as all hell. People stare at her, but no one dares speak to her until they've had at least three drinks themselves, that's how fucking intimidating she is. She's not drinking to get to some un-inhibited place; she already lives in that place. She's drinking because she needs to take the edge off; she's got so many existential thoughts going on in that mind of hers. She is the girl we most want to be.

And while it's fun to be this girl in a bar, it's even more fun to be her in the comfort of your own home. This way, you don't even have to wear a bra with your turtleneck.

Honestly, if you're coming home from a shit day and in the mood to make yourself an artisanal cocktail, this is the one to make. You can journal, you can read Joan Didion. You can also watch the Housewives. We're not judging. You do you. You'll only need one and soon enough you'll think: "You know what, I just don't have any more fucks to give." Turtleneck not required.

INGREDIENTS

1½ ounces gin

¾ ounce Campari

¾ ounce sweet vermouth

Twist of orange peel, for garnish

DIRECTIONS

- Combine the gin, Campari, and vermouth in a pint glass with ice.

- Stir with a spoon for 20 seconds.

- Strain into a chilled cocktail glass and garnish with the orange peel twist.

- Serve with no fucks whatsoever.

SERVES 1

HOT BODY HOT TODDY

MPB

They say when you're sick you can't drink, and it's definitely true, you probably shouldn't, except for when you have to. Like, if you're invited to a black-tie gala when you have pneumonia, or if you're marrying a prince during flu season, or if your boyfriend is bringing soup over and you want to have a fun night. When he sees you in an adorable pair of sick-pajamas sipping a hot toddy from a mug, his heart will melt.

Sometimes you just cannot put your life on hold when you're a little ill. You were invited to a party and you need to go, and you need to drink because you're young and socially anxious and not yet ready to compromise or truly worry about your health. We've got you. Go to your party and order a hot toddy. People will think you're interesting or Irish and it will be good for your throat. Also, your tolerance will be very low due to your bad immune system, so you're guaranteed a great night.

The hot toddy is also useful when you're hanging at home. You've been sick all week and you're sick of being sick? You need to get out of your head? This drink will raise your spirits, help you fall asleep, and probably allow you to more comfortably watch that movie. So whenever you have hot (fever) body, drink a hot toddy.

INGREDIENTS

1½ ounces whiskey, brandy, or bourbon

1 tablespoon honey

Juice of ½ lemon

1 cup hot water

Lemon wedge, whole star anise seed, and/or cinnamon stick, for garnish

DIRECTIONS

• Combine the liquor, honey, lemon juice, and hot water in a mug or a tumbler.

• Stir well and garnish with the lemon, star anise, and/or cinnamon stick.

• Serve hot.

SERVES 1

BAD BITCH MARGARITAS

MPB

Oftentimes, I'll order a "girly" drink while on a date or just hanging out with a dude, and then I'll apologize for myself. "God, this fruity drink is so lame, isn't it?"

And the guy will invariably say, "No, it's fine, you can drink whatever you want. You're a girl."

I really hate this. Please do not lower the coolness standards by which you judge my alcoholic beverage just because I am a woman. I want my drinks to be judged at the same level as those of my male counterparts.

The worst, though, is when I order a drink that I don't consider lame or girly, and a guy thinks it is. I am talking specifically about the margarita. The margarita is my go-to drink when I want to get toasted and have a good time, and not only at a Mexican restaurant. Tequila is an upper, and I need as much upper as I can get without taking actual pills.

Lately, the lady ordering a margarita has gotten a bad rap. I'm not going to name names, but someone out there who was on a reality TV show started something called, like, the Anorexic Marg for Morons, and while it tastes good, it's sort of ruined my life. I go out to a bar and I say, "Hi, can I please have a margarita with salt, but not too sweet . . . not too much simple syrup, please?"

"So you mean a skinny margarita," the trendy Los Angeles waiter will often reply.

"No, just not too sweet. This isn't about weight, you see. It's just about taste. Thanks," I say, and then pull out my boxing glove and punch the waiter in the face. "I would like a margarita, like my fucking dad orders, like Jack Kerouac would have ordered! Okay? It was cool before it was skinny. AAAGH!" By this point I am usually standing on the table giving a lecture about what a true margarita is, and what it means to me, and how the skinny margarita is not who I am and does not define me. After I feel I have spoken out to my heart's content, I bow and do a backflip off the table.

And then the guy I'm out with realizes I am cool and forgets everything he thought about me before.

BAD BITCH MARGARITAS

INGREDIENTS

1 lime, quartered

Kosher salt

2 ounces white tequila

1 ounce triple sec (or fresh orange juice)

1 ounce freshly squeezed lime juice (from about 2 limes)

½ ounce freshly squeezed lemon juice (from about ½ lemon)

1 cup ice, plus extra for serving

DIRECTIONS

- If you like margaritas served with salt, rub the outside rim of a glass with a lime quarter and lightly dip the glass rim-down into a plate of kosher salt.

- Combine the tequila, triple sec or orange juice, lime juice, lemon juice, and ice in a shaker and shake well to mix. (Or, for a blended margarita, puree in a blender until smooth.)

- Serve in the salt-rimmed glass (or in a regular glass, if preferred).

SERVES 1

SLUTTY/VIRGIN MARY

MPB

I've talked a lot about relationships I created in my mind or flirtations gone awry, but there was a time when I KNEW I felt something. Truly, I was positive of it and I was going to make something of it.

It started one night, when my friend Dan and I decided to have an adventure, by which I mean we went to a birthday party of a person we didn't know. We were bored and expecting nothing, but it turned out to be a great party in a beautiful house. The host, Max, was a cute, short, blond Jewish guy, and exactly my type: me! Odds were in my favor, as I was the only person at the party shorter than he was. He quickly became my party husband. We flirted while grilling steak outside together. We joked about how we had the same phenotype. We even shared a piece of cake. I was going to leave; he asked me to stay, and I did. Then, at the end of the night, he didn't even ask for my number. Of course, having lost not only a party husband but also a possible real husband, I cried in the Uber home. Now I know what it's like to go through a divorce.

Later, I found out that his ex-girlfriend had arrived at the party and he felt weird making a move in front of her. Okay, he was forgiven because to flirt with a girl all night long and then not even ask for a number is a crime not even acceptable during the Purge or the Hunger Games or the Divergent series. I paid no mind to the fact this ex-girlfriend was still around. I was going to make things work. I mean, we had been through so much. We owed it to ourselves to give this a chance.

A month later I was invited to another of his parties. I went, and the exact same thing happened. This time we shared a piece of pizza. Sharing food was "our thing," I guess. Lots of fun and flirting, but no move made. Again, I found out this scary ex-girlfriend had been there. Again, I paid her no mind. I also paid no mind to the fact that she was an artist and her paintings covered every wall in this guy's house. There are sometimes signs, if you look for signs.

A third chance arose. I was at my best friend's housewarming party. (Sidebar: I'm not invited to that many parties. I'm only writing about the times I have been.) I was toasted as can be when I heard that Max was having a casual gathering at his house. I turned to my friend as her party was dwindling down and told her I had to go. I had a mission. She understood. I was the star of my own life! I was not the funny best friend! And I was going to make something happen. (I'm only this confident under the influence.)

I played it perfectly, albeit drunk and falling. I hate dogs, but I flirted with Max's dog all night. I was petting it, snuggling with it, making cool jokes like "I really only come here for the dog. I really just want to fuck your dog." My greatest move was when I was standing in a circle with Max, Dan, and a guy Dan liked. I was like, "Max, can we go get a drink?" I was so smooth. "See what I did there?" I said to him after we'd left the other two guys alone. "They like each other."

"Good job, do you want to go out on the balcony?"

"Sure!"

He pushed me up against the side of his house and kissed me. Was a drunken make-out session what I had initially wanted? No, of course not, I had wanted a dinner date at the fanciest restaurant in all the land, but this was fairly hot and romantic, in its way. The party continued and we were now officially party married, but for real this time. I adopted the dog. A lawyer was involved, I swear. When everyone started shuffling out, I obviously stayed. I was moving in next week and needed to figure out which closet would be mine. Clearly just staying at someone's house is my party move. No time for hard to get.

We were on his couch; I was showing him my new rebellious ear piercings. Then we moved to the bedroom. Things heated up very quickly from there. Clothes off, etc. I mean, we were married, might as well consummate it. About ten minutes into this, I heard a banging on the front door. The banging got louder and finally a key turned in the lock.

A girl burst in screaming, "Hello? Hello! I know you're in here!" Meanwhile, in the bedroom, Max covered my mouth with his hand. "Don't say anything!" *What do you mean, Max? I'm dying to talk to this girl! She's my boo.* We tried to stay quiet so she'd just leave, but she refused. "I know you're in there. I'm coming in!"

He jumped up. "I'll be right back. Don't move."

"Okay, cool, I'll just chill here."

I figured I'd wait for her to go, and then I'd just bounce myself, but this girl would not leave. "I know there's someone in there!" Max just kept saying, "I didn't know you were coming. I didn't know you were coming." So, what, it would be cool for him to cheat if he *did* know she was coming? Was he even cheating? It still wasn't clear whether they were together or she was some crazy ex. I think they were "broken up, but still sleeping together"? They just kept going back and forth, and it didn't look like she would be leaving anytime soon. I decided I should try to fall asleep. That way, he would have to deal with me in his bed and would be very uncomfortable about it. Or they'd have to wake me up together and ask me to leave. Something good would happen. So there I was, snuggling away with the dog, when I

heard: "Does this girl know there's dried semen in there from last night?" *Okay, now it's time to go.* I jumped up. I put on my jeans and my bra. I couldn't find my shirt. *Fuck her, I'm going out there in a bra.*

"Hi," I said. "I'm Miranda. It's so nice to meet you. I just need to find my shirt and then I'm out of here."

"Me too," she said. "Should we share an Uber?"

I had to give her credit for the joke. "No, thanks!" I did kind of want someone to be like, *"Should we all stay?"* just so I could be outraged, but everyone was too self-aware for that. (In retrospect, should I have made the joke? Hmm . . .)

Finally she left, and I waited for a huge apology from this guy. He just stood there in shock, repeating, "I didn't know she was coming. I'm sorry. I'm sorry." Part of me wanted to be cool and say, "Hey, want to have a drink and tell me about it?" But then another part of me wanted to get the hell out of there. The insecure and strongest part of me wanted him to say, "I really like you, please stay." Of course, none of the above occurred.

The next morning I woke up hungover and laughing. I wasn't offended, just kind of like, *How the hell did that happen to me?* I was thankful, actually. It's important to have something interesting happen to you every couple of months so you have something to talk about when you go out to dinner. I dined on this story for weeks.

It would be fine if this story ended here, but it didn't. A month later, I got the apology from Max that I had been waiting for. I agreed to let him take me out. "A lot of great relationships start with something insane," I told myself. This was a moment when I had all the power. This guy had to really make it up to me! My friends said, "Cherish this moment, Miranda." And instead, I lost it all immediately and slept with him that night. To make matters worse, I slept with him outside, in a construction site, and it was my idea. He texted me a picture of the construction site later that week, but never responded after that.

I continued to sleep with him whenever we ran into each other for a year. Never once did he ask me out again or make me feel actually special. He'd tell me he'd listened to my podcast just to hear my voice and all my self-respect would go out the window. Once, I slept with him the night before my birthday and told him he absolutely had to spend the night. "I won't think we're together," I said. "I just don't want to wake up alone on my birthday." The next morning he was gone.

That was the final straw . . . until the next time I texted him. He is the only guy I have ever texted anything remotely like "You up?" to. There's just no shame left to be had in front of him. After a certain point, I finally deleted his number. (While editing, I had to check to make sure I actually deleted this number. I'm so proud to tell you I did. This wasn't a lie!)

To this day, though, he is my Bloody Mary guy, because whenever I wake up having seen him, I need to forget it. Sometimes you just have to admit you're too hungover to move. More important, sometimes when you're too ashamed to live with what happened the night before, it's not a bad idea to invite a friend over for a Bloody Mary and laugh about it, or try to laugh about it. Or to forgive yourself for being in your midtwenties and acting like a college student. Please join me for a Bloody Mary right about now.

Question: Should I go back and steal his dog? Think about it.

SLUTTY/VIRGIN MARY

INGREDIENTS

4 ounces tomato juice

2 ounces vodka

Juice of ½ lemon

½ teaspoon sriracha, or more to taste

½ teaspoon Worcestershire sauce

¼ teaspoon grated horseradish

⅛ teaspoon celery salt

Assorted garnishes (see list at right)

DIRECTIONS

• Combine all the ingredients in a mixing glass.

• Add several ice cubes and stir to combine and chill.

• Strain into an ice-filled pint glass and garnish with any of the ingredients listed at right.

GARNISHES

Celery sticks

Lemon wedges

Lime wedges

Cherry tomatoes

Olives

Sliced radishes

Kimchi

Pickled or cocktail onions

Sliced pickles

Cornichons

Marinated mushrooms

Pickled asparagus

SERVES 1

CHAPTER 7

Swipe Left, Cook Right

Navigating the world of modern romance can be fucking impossible. Social media, the rise of the throuple, and, frankly, porn make it very difficult for us to know what the fuck is going on. We want a foolproof GPS to guide us and tell us to swerve left when there's a commitmentphobe in our path. The technology just isn't there yet. Until it is, we want to help you. We can't give you a set of rules, because we don't think they exist, but we can give you some tools to make dating a little bit easier. And these are delicious tools!

At the time of publication, Gabi was recently married, and Miranda was still a hot fucking mess weeping audibly over a man-child during spin class. (Spin class is a great place to weep. People think you're just working very hard.) We tell you this to let you know that we're two women at different stages of our romantic lives, who can probably sympathize with some of what you're going through. You can read every book and take every piece of your friends' advice, but at the end of the day you just have to put yourself out there, feel a lot, and experience it all. That's the only way to find out exactly who and what will make you happy.

Whether you're frantically pacing around your apartment waiting for a text or madly in love, we've got the recipes to help you through it. We've got a chicken that will make any conquest fall at your feet with love. If you don't get a proposal at the end of the meal, we'll give you your money back. (No, obviously, this is a lie. See chapter titled "Broke AF.") And don't worry; we have also included plenty of recipes for the times when nothing is going your way. I Created a Relationship in My Mind Cupcakes are just perfect for eating your feelings on the couch while internet-stalking your crush's ex-wife's cousin on her Pilates retreat. Finally, when you're ready for revenge that won't get you arrested, our Eat Your Enemy Crispy Treats will do just the trick. Bitches be crazy, though; you've probably already keyed at least thirty-five cars.

It's true what the Supremes said about how you can't hurry love, but we promise you that most of these recipes are ready to eat in a hurry (except for Texting Jitters Jam, which is strategically designed to keep you occupied for a long period of time). And unlike dating, we promise every last one of these recipes will end well. —GLM & MPB

A DATE WITH THE DEVIL('S) FOOD CAKE WITH EASY CHOCOLATE FROSTING

GLM & MPB

We love online dating (Gabi met Evan on OkCupid), but we also know that it can be pretty damn weird. Before online dating, if you had agreed to go out with someone, you'd likely have met them before. You'd smelled their pheromones and deemed them human and acceptable to have drinks with, or maybe you'd been set up by a respectable-ish third party. Today we swipe right and leave the house hoping for decent conversation and a touch of good chem. A first date is really just an interview to see if you can get slightly drunk and make out with someone, right? We think that's a good way of looking at it.

A few months before she met Evan, Gabi showed up to a date with a guy who was literally a foot shorter than he purported to be. There's a ceiling for dating-profile lying, and that ceiling is shorter than a foot. (It's probably a four-inch ceiling.)

Miranda, meanwhile, arrived to meet a guy only to find out he had double-booked her. She went up to him and said, "Hi, are you John?" He looked at her on his right and another girl on his left and literally sprinted out of the bar. She was left to have drinks with a girl who was basically her twin, but, like, a hot yoga instructor version of her. (She did, however, end up getting a free breathwork class out of the thing. It's not for her.)

Look, even online dating success stories are usually preceded by a lot of terrible online dating stories. But even on those awful nights when the guy is lame, the drinks are weak, and the conversation is awkward, you deserve a rich, chocolaty treat. You showered. You put on a dress. You wasted some witty well-crafted texts on an idiot. You took a chance, right? No risk, no reward. No devil, no devil's food cake.

A DATE WITH THE DEVIL('S) FOOD CAKE

INGREDIENTS

For the cakes

¾ cup unsweetened cocoa powder (not hot cocoa mix)

½ cup boiling water

3 cups all-purpose flour or cake flour

1 teaspoon baking soda

½ teaspoon salt

3 sticks unsalted butter (1½ cups), at room temperature, plus more for pans

2¼ cups granulated sugar

1 tablespoon vanilla extract

4 large eggs, lightly beaten

1 cup milk

For the Easy Chocolate Frosting

1 stick unsalted butter (½ cup), at room temperature

6 tablespoons unsweetened cocoa powder

½ cup whole milk

2 teaspoons vanilla extract

4 cups powdered sugar

NOTE: You could instead use a couple of cans of prepared chocolate frosting. You'll need about 6 cups.

DIRECTIONS

Make the cakes

- Sift the cocoa powder into a medium bowl, then whisk in the boiling water. Set aside to cool.

- Arrange two racks in the center of the oven and preheat to 350°F.

- Butter three 8 × 2-inch round cake pans and line their bottoms with parchment.

- In a large bowl, sift together the flour, baking soda, and salt.

- In the bowl of an electric mixer fitted with the paddle attachment, beat the butter at low speed until light and fluffy.

- Gradually beat in the granulated sugar, 3 to 4 minutes, scraping down the sides twice.

- Beat in the vanilla extract.

- Pour in the eggs a little at a time, beating between each addition until the batter is no longer slick, scraping down the sides twice.

- Whisk the milk into the cooled cocoa mixture.

- With the mixer on low speed, alternately add the flour and cocoa mixtures to the batter, a little of each at a time, starting and ending with the flour mixture.

- Divide the batter evenly among the three prepared pans.

- Bake for 35 to 45 minutes, rotating the pans once or twice for even baking, until a toothpick or cake tester inserted in the center of each pan comes out clean.

- Transfer cakes to wire racks and let cool for 15 minutes.

- Gently remove the cakes from their pans, and let cool completely.

Make the Easy Chocolate Frosting

- Melt the butter in a large microwave-safe bowl in the microwave. Whisk in the cocoa powder.

- Add the milk and vanilla extract and whisk until frothy. Make sure that the cocoa powder has completely dissolved.

- In a stand mixer with a beater attachment, with a hand mixer, or by hand with a whisk (and a strong arm!), work the powdered sugar into the liquid a little at a time until fully incorporated.

- The frosting should be thick but spreadable. If it is runny, add more powdered sugar; if too stiff, work in a teaspoon of milk.

- Use immediately, or let cool in the fridge, then whip again until fluffy.

NOTE: This frosting will keep for several days in the fridge, but make sure it's tightly covered. It will dry out and form a thin crust if exposed to air.

Assemble the cake

- Remove the parchment from the bottoms of the cakes.

- Select the prettiest layer; use this one for the top of the cake.

- Place one cake layer on a serving platter. Spread 1½ cups of the frosting over the top.

- Add the second cake layer, and spread with another 1½ cups of frosting on top.

- Top with the third cake layer. Cover the top and sides of the cake with the remaining 3 cups of frosting. Slice and serve.

- If you're crying, the tears will only make the cake more moist. (But don't cry, you deserve better.)

SERVES 8 TO 10

I CREATED A RELATIONSHIP IN MY MIND CUPCAKES

MPB

Hello, you little cupcakes with overactive imaginations.

I have a dessert and story for you!

I've created many a relationship in my mind. There was the time a celebrity favorited three of my tweets and I thought we were in love. Or when I had coffee with a guy once a week to discuss his life (therapy) and thought it was going to turn into a marriage, and hopefully a long, strung-out artistic relationship before that. I mean, I have five pretend relationships happening in my mind right now, and fifteen Snapchat affairs that I have to keep track of as well. It's so hard!

Every now and then, I forget that these relationships are in my mind and I believe they are real. I fall in love with the idea of someone, as we all do. Once I was very positive I had found the one, or a one, or a summer one. I was doing a boring internship and had plenty of time to let my mind wander. I got very friendly with one of the other interns, a guy named Sam. We

ate lunch together every day and hung out almost every weekend at the beach. Slowly our relationship started to get flirtier. I made sure to wear a V-neck every day. That's how I knew it was real. There was even a little bit of drunken snuggling in the backseat of a cab once. This, combined with my surefire analysis of his psyche (he'd never be as smart or successful as his father and therefore hated himself and I could save him), made me certain we were basically a couple.

One night he had a party at his house. Slowly everyone shuffled out and I, drunkenly, decided not to go. My friends wanted to go. I ignored all their texts and basically forced them to leave without me. This was my night.

Soon, when almost everyone was gone, Sam noticed I was still there. He came over and invited me to spend the night, but not at all in the way I would have liked him to. He said something like: "Well, it's very late. I feel sorry for you. And all your friends are gone. Do you need to stay? Did you come alone?" Hopeful, I said yes. Sam grabbed my hand and walked me to his bedroom. Here it was. We were finally going to consummate our summerlong flirtation. It was *The Notebook*, but drunk and slobbery and falling over.

He turned the knob to his room, where we found ten dudes sharing two twin beds, and a few more on the floor. It was a slumber party for twenty-two-year-old college boys. Some of the guys were kind enough to get off the second bed and Sam and I shared it. Then there were knocks at the door. More of their friends were trying to file in. Joy! My night of love! Finally, someone took a stand. Sam's best friend, Adam, valiantly said, "No, we hate those guys. Miranda, can you please make some believable sex noises so these assholes think you're fucking Sam?" Sam was dead asleep at this point. This inquiry, while slightly offensive, did prove to me that Adam noticed I was a girl. I was happy about this. Wanting to save the night, I accepted the challenge. This seemed like something that would happen in a movie, so I had to say yes. Also, I felt I could probably turn a few of the guys on with my special noises, and I needed to raise my self-esteem however I could in that exact moment.

I was successful. The boys were turned away. Everyone cheered for me and then went to bed.

I rested my head next to snoring Sam and took off my bra just in case he snuggled me in the night. I think I stroked his hair or something as I lay next to him. He was drunk, and I wanted to take care of him, braless.

In the morning, he woke up surprised to find me next to him and immediately offered to drive me to my friend's house. We were silent in the car. I do think there might have been something between us that summer, but it was probably just friendship.

When I got home the next night, I cried. I was all alone. My parents were out of town and I was staying with them. The weekend hangover was settling in and I realized there had never been a real relationship at all. There was only the idea of him, and that is a sad thing to lose. It's a really sad thing to lose. Fantasies sometimes keep us going. Fantasies are the best drugs.

What I needed on that Sunday night was something sweet to make the comedown a little bit easier and an activity to distract myself. What I needed was to make these cupcakes. And I wish I had.

I CREATED A RELATIONSHIP IN MY MIND CUPCAKES

INGREDIENTS

2 cups granulated sugar

4 eggs

2½ cups all-purpose flour

1 cup milk (any fat percentage will work, or use nondairy milk)

¾ cup vegetable oil

2¼ teaspoons baking powder

1 teaspoon vanilla extract

¼ cup raspberry preserves (you can make your own Texting Jitters Jam on page 222)

Easy Chocolate Frosting (see page 216), Cream Cheese Frosting (see page 164), or prepared icing of your choice

Fresh raspberries, for garnish

DIRECTIONS

• Preheat the oven to 350°F.

• Line two 12-cup cupcake pans with paper liners (or grease the cups with butter or cooking spray).

• In a large mixing bowl, beat the sugar and eggs together with an electric mixer until slightly thickened, about 1 minute. Alternately, use a whisk and beat for 2 to 3 minutes.

• Add the flour, milk, oil, baking powder, and vanilla extract and beat for another minute, just until the batter is smooth and creamy. Fill the prepared cups two-thirds of the way.

• Place a teaspoon of raspberry preserves into each cupcake and swirl it with a spoon.

• Bake for 30 to 45 minutes, or until the tops are golden and a toothpick poked into the center comes out clean.

• Let the cupcakes cool completely in the pan, then frost as desired. Top each one with a fresh raspberry.

• Go outside. Talk to a real human.

MAKES 2 DOZEN CUPCAKES

TEXTING JITTERS JAM

MPB

T he following recipe will occupy your hands for quite some time. This is so you cannot touch your phone.

We know times are tough for you right now. You've just sent a text message to someone with whom you are either romantically involved or wishing to be so. First of all, congratulations on sending that message. It's good to go after the things you want. You regret 65 percent of the texts you don't send. (This is a made-up statistic.) Even if you are just confirming plans for the night ahead, sending a text can raise your heart rate from stable resting to cocaine frenzy.

Does sending the first text really make you lose all your power?

When will these crazy games end?

Do we even want them to end, or do we love the drama?

Do I really look like that?

Where is my skinny mirror? Ah, blessed skinny mirror! There you are. My one true love!

We know where you're at right now.

When I first got AOL, every time I instant-messaged a boy, I would run around my family's apartment screaming with panic. (I still do this, but now it's more related to professional emails or weighing myself.)

I also happen to know that Gabi has been with Evan for more than five years, and she still gets "Why isn't he texting back?" anxiety when he takes more than ten minutes to respond to her.

Anyhow, save yourself and your heart! Take three deep breaths, throw your phone into a ditch (or just turn it off), and make this jam.

"Jam? Really?" you ask. "I'm, like, a cool normal lady, not some weirdo making jam all day." We say yes. This jam will stop you from spiraling out of control while waiting for a response to a text message. It also will serve as a cool gift for that birthday lunch you're going to tomorrow or next week.

If you put your jam into a hip jar and make it your own, you're really reappropriating the whole jam game, you know? That's our jam.

Our advice: FIGHT. THE. SPIRAL. Make jam instead. You have to do something with your hands so you can forget about your head and heart for a little bit. If you don't hear from this person by the time you're done with this recipe, get rid of them. No movie is this long and they are being evasive and weird.

NOTE: You will need six ½-pint mason jars with fitted lids for this recipe.

TEXTING JITTERS JAM

INGREDIENTS

2 pounds fresh raspberries or strawberries (or a mix)

1¼ cups sugar

Juice of ½ lemon (about 3 tablespoons)

2 tablespoons balsamic vinegar

¼ teaspoon pepper

Pinch of salt

DIRECTIONS

- Place the berries and sugar in a mixing bowl and stir to combine.

- Let sit for 1 hour.

- Using soap and hot water, wash six ½-pint mason jars (or equivalent) with fitted lids and sealing rings.

- Fill a large pot with water and bring it to a boil.

- Submerge the jars and lids in the boiling water and boil for 10 minutes.

- Use clean tongs to remove and let dry completely on clean dish towels.

- Combine the sugar-raspberry mixture and the lemon juice in a medium pot over medium-high heat and bring to a boil.

- Reduce heat to medium and let simmer until the jam begins to jell, about 30 minutes.

- Add the vinegar, pepper, and salt to the jam. Stir well and simmer for another 5 minutes, then remove the jam from heat.

- Ladle the jam into the prepared mason jars and seal the lids tightly.

- Submerge the sealed jars in the boiling water for 15 minutes to form a good seal (do this in batches if your pot isn't big enough to boil all six jars at once). Remove and set aside to cool.

- The jam may be used once it is cooled, but it is best after at least 24 hours. If left sealed, it will keep for up to 2 years.

- If you haven't gotten a text by now, delete this person from your contacts. They are the worst.

MAKES 6 HALF-PINT JARS

BAD SEX BAKED POTATOES

GLM & MPB

Ugh, this is the worst. As if it weren't bad enough that you just had horrible prolonged (or, in some cases, not nearly prolonged enough) physical contact, now you have all kinds of anxiety about it. You're asking yourself all sorts of questions like:

1. Is it going to give you a yeast infection? Or something worse?
2. Was it because of them?
3. Was it because of you?
4. Can it get better with this person or is it over?
5. Is that really the face they make when they orgasm? Is my orgasm face just as bad?
6. Did I do it too early and ruin everything?
7. Have I lost all the power in this relationship?

In our experience, the answers are typically as follows:

1. No, but make sure to go pee right afterward anyway.
2. Probably yes.
3. Probably also yes, but only because you were nervous.
4. It can get better, but sometimes really, really bad sex is indicative of the fact that there's a mismatch somehow, be it emotional or biological.
5. Yes. And no! You look hot as hell, but go practice in the mirror. You can definitely control how you look when you come.
6. Probably also yes.
7. God! Who knows? Maybe. Who knows? Case-by-case basis.

Whatever the reason, bad sex can leave you feeling empty and unsatisfied. Go home and warm your heart (and your belly) with a cheesy twice-baked potato. You deserve more. Bad sex doesn't even mean the sex was actually bad; it can be that a false sense of intimacy was created and now you've gone home and you're alone. You were vulnerable with someone who didn't deserve it. And it feels terrible. It was too soon to do that, but try not to beat yourself up. You've learned a lesson, and that's all you can hope for at this stage in your life. Maybe next time you'll act differently, or maybe you'll do the same thing ten more times until you finally change.

BAD SEX BAKED POTATOES

INGREDIENTS

2 medium russet potatoes, skin on, scrubbed

1 tablespoon extra-virgin olive oil

½ medium onion, chopped

1 clove garlic, chopped

1 cup chopped kale (dinosaur or Tuscan; about 2–3 kale leaves)

¾ cup shredded cheddar cheese (jack, Muenster, or fontina also work)

1 tablespoon unsalted butter

Salt and pepper

DIRECTIONS

• Preheat the oven to 400°F.

• Line a rimmed baking sheet with foil and set aside.

• Pierce each potato several times with a fork. Place on a baking sheet.

• Roast the potatoes for 40 to 45 minutes, until a fork easily slides into the flesh.

• While potatoes roast, heat the olive oil in a large frying pan over medium heat. Add the onion and garlic and cook, stirring occasionally, for 3 to 4 minutes, until they begin to soften.

• Add the kale and cook, stirring occasionally, for 7 to 8 minutes, until the kale is very wilted. Remove from heat and transfer the vegetables to a mixing bowl.

• When the potatoes are ready, take them out of the oven and let them cool for 5 minutes. (Leave the oven on.)

• Slice the potatoes in half lengthwise and use a spoon to scoop out the cooked flesh. (You may need to leave a thin layer of flesh close to the skin to keep the skin from tearing.)

• Place the scooped-out potato flesh into the mixing bowl with the onion-kale mixture. Set the skins aside (you'll use them later).

• Add most of the cheese (reserve a few pinches to top the potatoes) and the butter to the bowl and use a fork to mash the mixture together. Season with salt and pepper to taste.

• Divide the mixture between the empty potato skins and top each with a pinch of the reserved shredded cheese. Place the stuffed potatoes on the lined baking sheet.

• Bake for 18 to 20 minutes, or until the cheese on top begins to bubble and brown.

• Serve immediately.

SERVES 2 (YOU CAN SAVE THE SECOND ONE FOR LUNCH TOMORROW . . . OR EAT BOTH.)

THIRD DATE DUMPLINGS

GLM

There's plenty of conventional wisdom about the proper order of operations for a new relationship: when a first kiss should be, when first-time sex should take place, and when you might meet each other's friends. But to my knowledge, there isn't much out there about when it's a good idea to introduce cooking into a budding relationship.

When I first began working with food professionally, I loved the thrill of impressing men I was dating (or trying to date) with a home-cooked meal right out of the gate. Who doesn't love a delicious meal cooked solely for him by a girl doing her best to look cute? (Anyone who has chopped onions while wearing mascara can attest that this is not easy.)

At first, this would seem like a great idea. Praising my culinary prowess, my dates would

lick their plates clean, and if I was lucky, offer to help with the dishes. But then one of two scenarios would transpire:

1. I'd never hear from the guy again.

2. We'd continue seeing each other, but it would become expected that I keep cooking. Eager to be loved, I would confuse my suitor's affection for my Bolognese sauce with affection for me. Rather than go out on dates, I'd continue whipping up gourmet meals for the two of us. But a tiny seed of resentment would be planted . . . one that no amount of dishwashing could temper. Eventually, I'd end it.

When I met Evan, I didn't want to make this mistake again. After our first date, in a bar, and our second, a picnic in a park where we got tipsy on cheap wine and shared our first kiss, I came up with a way that he and I could cook together.

My thinking was that if we worked on our meal as a team, we could share in the fun of eating the fruits of our labors, plus, it wouldn't accidentally establish an expectation that I was the sole cook in the relationship.

Because I didn't know what his culinary skill level was, I knew I had to come up with something simple. I didn't want to overwhelm him or make a big mess that we'd have to clean up afterward, but I also knew I wanted something with a fair amount of hands-on time, so it felt like an actual activity. Finally, I figured it out: homemade dumplings.

I bought dumpling skins at my local Asian grocery store (if you don't live near an Asian specialty market, look for wonton or potsticker skins near the tofu in your supermarket), and we made a simple vegetarian filling. Together, we sat at my kitchen table, rolling the dumplings, talking, laughing, and drinking beer all the while. Cleanup afterward was simple, which was a good thing, because the moment we each ate our last dumpling, we moved to the couch to make out.

THIRD DATE DUMPLINGS

INGREDIENTS

2 large sweet potatoes, peeled and diced

1½ tablespoons soy sauce, plus more for dipping

2 teaspoons toasted sesame oil

4 green onions, thinly sliced

1 clove garlic, minced

1 (½-inch) piece ginger, peeled and grated

2 teaspoons sriracha or other Asian chili sauce (more or less to taste)

30 small round dumpling wrappers

Coconut or other vegetable oil, for frying

Rice vinegar, for dipping

DIRECTIONS

- Bring a pot of salted water to a boil and cook the sweet potatoes until very tender, about 10 minutes.

- Drain the sweet potatoes and rinse with cold water until cool to the touch. Transfer to a mixing bowl.

- Use the back of a fork to mash the sweet potatoes until smooth. Add the soy sauce, sesame oil, green onions (reserve a pinch for the sauce), garlic, ginger, and Asian chili sauce (check with your date about spice tolerance before adding that last one).

- To assemble the dumplings, lay a dumpling wrapper flat on your work surface. Brush the edges lightly with water (use a clean finger or a small pastry brush).

- Place about 2 teaspoons of the sweet potato mixture in the center of the wrapper. Fold the wrapper in half and make 5 to 6 small pleats as you seal the edges together, pinching gently to ensure total closure.

- Transfer the folded dumpling onto a floured baking sheet or platter and repeat with the remaining filling and wrappers.

- To cook the dumplings, heat a couple of tablespoons of the oil in a large frying pan that has a fitted lid over medium heat. (Set the lid within easy reach.)

- Working in batches, arrange the dumplings close to one another (but not touching) in the pan, flat side down, and cook for 2 to 3 minutes, until a golden crust begins to develop on the bottom.

- Carefully pour ⅛ cup water over the dumplings, then cover the pan quickly and let steam for about 3 minutes.

- Remove the lid and let the dumplings aerate until the excess water is cooked away and the bottoms become crisp again.

- Transfer the cooked dumplings to a serving platter and repeat with the remaining uncooked dumplings, adding more oil as needed.

- Serve immediately with a half-and-half mixture of soy sauce and rice vinegar with the reserved green onions for dipping.

SERVES 2, WITH LEFTOVERS

I'M CHILL, BUT WE'RE OBVIOUSLY EXCLUSIVE? FISH TACOS WITH MANGO-AVOCADO SALSA

MPB

Trying to be the "cool girl" is exhausting.

I once waited five months to have "the talk" with a guy I was seeing. I wanted to seem like the kind of girl who just didn't give a fuck, who had eighty-seven other people texting her for dates, but also I was truly afraid he would just say he didn't want more and leave me in the dust. He'd want to remain free as a bird that couldn't commit to his flock. Frankly, I wasn't sure what I wanted either, so when I set out to "have the talk," I was very blasé about the whole thing.

One night I invited him over for a fancy dinner and planned to will him into realizing we were a couple. He'd buy the booze. I'd make a roast and wear an apron. We'd feel feelings. Our eyes would lock in an intense moment and I would say something romantic along the lines of, "So I'm, like, your girlfriend, right? Because my sister is getting married and I'd like to have a date."

"Yes," he would respond. "I am completely mad for you and how you could think otherwise for even one second is beyond me. Also, I love weddings."

This didn't happen.

Instead I got very frustrated with an impossible meal. My roast was burnt and my heart was racing. We got totally bombed because there was no food, had sex, showered, and showed up late to my best friend's birthday party. At the party, drunker, I couldn't control myself. I pushed him into a room and said, "What the hell are we doing?" He asked why I was bringing it up now, at a party. I acknowledged my immaturity and added that I just couldn't take it anymore. He commended me on waiting so long. He was impressed! That said, he wouldn't call me his girlfriend quite yet. He did tell me that his parents knew my name, and that was enough for me, at least in that moment.

The first lesson is regarding food. If you're trying to be blasé about the whole thing, you can set the tone with the food. Tacos are chill. Surfers eat them on the beach and stuff. Why make an impossible roast to try to impress someone you're already dating?

The second lesson here is: If you're not that chill, don't pretend to be. Your feelings are precious and you should take note of them, I hear. They're probably going to come out sooner or later, and if they don't, they will fester and make you feel even worse (I hear this too). There are no chill girls, only chill flannel shirts. You should know what you want and go after it.

Gabi knows how to do that. Gabi is badass in that way. That's why she makes Steak Your Claim Steak, and I make casual coy tacos. Let's say her steak at right is for when you're sure, and you want an answer; these tacos are for when you're a little more wishy-washy and want things to work themselves out naturally, or for when you're a scared baby.

FISH TACOS WITH MANGO-AVOCADO SALSA

INGREDIENTS

2 roma tomatoes, diced

1 avocado, diced

1 mango, diced

½ red onion, diced

½ jalapeño, seeded and finely diced

1 small bunch cilantro, chopped

Juice of ½ lime

Salt

½ cup IPA beer (we like Lagunitas or Speakeasy's Big Daddy)

⅔ cup all-purpose flour, plus more for dusting fish

½ pound red snapper fillets (2–3 small fillets)

Vegetable oil, for frying

6 corn tortillas

NOTE: Beer-battered fish tacos are a classic. They're typically made with a light beer, such as Corona, but we're much bigger fans of darker, hoppier IPAs.

DIRECTIONS

- In a mixing bowl, combine the tomato, avocado, mango, onion, jalapeño, cilantro, lime juice, and a pinch of salt to make a salsa. Stir and set aside.

- Combine the beer, flour, and a pinch of salt in a bowl. Whisk until a smooth batter is achieved. Set aside.

- Cut the snapper fillets into 3-inch pieces, removing small bones if possible.

- Pour a little flour onto a plate. Lightly dredge the fish pieces in the flour, shaking off the excess. Set aside.

- Fill a deep skillet with vegetable oil to a depth of 1 inch. Heat the oil over high heat. Move the floured fish and the batter near the stove.

- Dip the floured fish pieces into the batter, ensuring each piece is fully coated and excess drips off.

- Fry the fish pieces, a few at a time, until golden brown and crisp on one side. Use metal tongs or a metal spatula to flip them and cook on the other side.

- Remove the fish pieces carefully and drain on paper towels.

- To assemble the tacos, top each corn tortilla with a few pieces of fish and a couple of large spoonfuls of the salsa. Serve immediately.

MAKES 6 TACOS

STEAK YOUR CLAIM

GLM

Regardless of your relationship status, you should have a fabulous steak recipe in your repertoire. It's so simple to cook a steak right, yet so many do it wrong. (Are you baking your steak? Stop fucking doing that right now. You'll never develop a proper crust on it and it will dry out. You are better than that.) Steak can be a little pricey, but fortunately, you need little more than a baked potato and a fresh or cooked vegetable to make it a full meal.

And when you need to have a DTR conversation (that's "define the relationship," one of my favorite acronyms), being able to throw together a badass steak is extremely helpful.

Picture this: You've been seeing each other for a month or two. The sex is good. Your potential partner is smart, sexy, and loves going down on you. And yet, it's still not totally clear what exactly this thing is. But you know what you want it to be.

You could stay quiet and hope the other person will bring it up eventually. Maybe they  will, but maybe they are also scared to bring it up. Or maybe they're not really interested in anything serious. In any case, you've got to put yourself out there, no matter what lies beyond. You have to stake your claim.

Like a well-executed DTR, the proper cooking of a steak must be timed well. Don't cook it very far in advance of serving. You want to pull it out of the pan, let it rest for about five minutes, then slice and serve it. If you let it sit for too long, the middle will overcook and what could have been a tender, juicy interior will turn tough and dry (sort of like you if you put this DTR off for much longer).

On the flip side (steak-cooking pun fully intended), if you don't let the steak rest and serve it too early, it may be bloody and raw inside. The juices will run all over your plate, and the meat will again be dry, since it didn't have that crucial resting period. It's a tricky business.

Here's the best plan: Invite your fuck buddy / date / more-than-friends friend over for dinner. Have the compound butter made and waiting in the fridge. Get your pan hot.

When your intended arrives, pour them a glass of red wine and say, "Oh, let me just throw the steak on and then we can eat." Be very low-key and chill as you salt and pepper your piece of meat. Let your "friend" enjoy the unmistakable fragrance of cooking beef. Then, just as the steak finishes, pull it out of the pan. Melt the compound butter over it and let it rest. Breathe. You're smooth, like compound butter. Like a good rib eye.

Then pull out a sharp knife, slice that buttery steak, serve it up, and stake your fucking claim. You got this.

STEAK YOUR CLAIM

INGREDIENTS

For the compound butter

3 tablespoons unsalted butter, at room temperature

1 clove garlic, minced

1 tablespoon fresh herbs (parsley, cilantro, rosemary, oregano, thyme, or a combination), chopped

Pinch each of salt and pepper

For the steak

1 tablespoon extra-virgin olive oil

1 (18- to 20-ounce) boneless rib eye steak, 1 inch to 1½ inches thick

Salt and pepper

DIRECTIONS

Make the compound butter

- In a small bowl, stir together the butter, garlic, herbs, salt, and pepper until completely mixed. Refrigerate until ready to use.

Make the steak

- Heat a griddle or frying pan (preferably cast iron) over medium-high heat. Brush it with the olive oil.

- Sprinkle the steak liberally with salt and pepper on both sides.

- Cook the steak for 4 to 4½ minutes on each side (longer to cook it past medium-rare).

- After cooking, transfer the steak to a cutting board and top it with the compound butter.

- Let it rest for at least 5 minutes.

- Slice the steak and serve immediately.

SERVES 2

I'M READY TO SLEEP WITH YOU CHOCOLATE MOUSSE

MPB

D o you remember when sleeping with someone new for the first time was special? A time when there was no alcohol involved, or if any, just Champagne, and you were in a hotel room with your one true love, and it was magical? Or maybe you'd just gotten married to your vampire husband, who'd promised to fuck you once before he turned you? And he'd taken you all the way to his vampire mom's private island just to do it! That's how exciting it is to him! That's what a big deal this first time is!

I don't remember this time. I remember a time when it was the third date and I was drunk and wanted to see if there was bed chem. I remember a time when I was totally wasted and rambling on about how where I was on my menstrual cycle would allow us to have unprotected sex, even though I wasn't on the pill. I remember a time when I thought, *Fuck it, might as well. I want you to like me.*

Well! I want to go back to the other time! So here's an idea: Make a special dessert that says, "Hey, sexy, I'm rad and ready. Wanna eff?" Be cool, though. Serve it after dinner, in a jokey way.

This dessert is rich, indulgent, and, yes, sexy. But when it comes to combining food and sex (something we don't have much experience with, but we want cool food-sex girls to buy this book), practicality is where it's at.

Crème brûlée, for example, is not a good postsex dessert, because it requires gently burning sugar with a kitchen torch—not a great idea when you're naked. But this gorgeous, creamy mousse can be prepared prebooty, spooned into goblets or wineglasses, and stored in the fridge until it's ready to serve. And walking to the fridge to retrieve goblets of creamy whipped dark chocolate mousse?

That you most definitely should do naked.

I'M READY TO SLEEP WITH YOU CHOCOLATE MOUSSE

INGREDIENTS

¾ cup semisweet chocolate, coarsely chopped (or use the equivalent chocolate chips)

14 ounces heavy cream, chilled

3 large egg whites

⅛ cup sugar

Sweetened whipped cream, for garnish (optional)

Shaved bittersweet chocolate, for garnish (optional)

DIRECTIONS

- Fill a small saucepan with tap water to a depth of about 2 inches. Cover with a heatproof bowl to create a double boiler. Bring the water to a low simmer over high heat and place the chocolate in the bowl, stirring until melted. (Alternately, melt the chocolate in a microwave-safe bowl in the microwave.)

- Turn off the heat and let stand.

- Beat the cream in a large mixing bowl until it forms soft peaks, 7 to 8 minutes (we like to use an electric beater for this, but you can do it by hand if you don't have one). Set aside.

- In a separate mixing bowl, whip the egg whites to soft peaks (again, with an electric beater or by hand). This should take 7 to 8 minutes.

- Gradually add the sugar to the egg whites and continue whipping until peaks form.

- Add the melted chocolate to the whipped egg whites.

- When the chocolate is almost completely incorporated, fold in the whipped heavy cream.

- Cover the mousse and refrigerate until set, about 1 hour.

- Divide the mousse between 2 wineglasses or cups and top with the sweetened whipped cream and shaved chocolate, if desired.

SERVES 2

MANIPULATION MAC AND CHEESE

GLM

When I was twenty-three, I made fresh gnocchi for a super-good-looking but kind of stupid guy I was dating. Like the true gem he was, he stood over me in the kitchen, wrinkling his nose and furrowing his brows at my every move.

"That's not how my mom does it," he said. "She doesn't use a food processor. She does it all by hand. And her gnocchi are amazing." Never mind the fact that I was twenty-three and making fucking gnocchi, from scratch.

I ignored him and concentrated on the burdensome task of peeling, boiling, and mashing potatoes and mixing them with just enough flour so the dough could be handled—but not so much that it became dense. When the gnocchi were finally complete and we sat down at my lovingly set kitchen table to eat, he took a bite, paused for a long time, and said, "These taste . . . different from my mom's."

Needless to say, it was our last date.

We can learn two things from this story. The first is that anyone who is bringing up their mother's cooking and implying that you are doing something wrong while you're generously cooking for them is not worth your time. The second is that childhood memories of food are powerful, and if handled carefully, they can be exploited for your benefit. Think about some of your favorite foods. Sure, some of them may be more sophisticated delicacies you encountered as an adult, but chances are that many of them are dishes you ate as a young child, prepared lovingly for you by your parents. Even more likely is that one of those foods is creamy, carby mac and cheese. And guess what—it's probably a childhood favorite of that hottie whose pants you're trying to get into too.

This utterly perfect baked mac and cheese is the real deal, likely to inspire happy memories of simpler times. You can class it up with a crisp green salad and a glass of cold white wine, or you can go old school and serve it with carrot sticks and apple juice.

And if anyone tries to tell you you're doing it wrong, tell them to get the hell out of your kitchen. More mac for you.

MANIPULATION MAC AND CHEESE

INGREDIENTS

8 ounces dried macaroni elbows (or other small-cut pasta)

3 tablespoons unsalted butter, plus more for the pan

3 tablespoons all-purpose flour

2 cups whole milk (this is not the time for low-fat)

1/4 teaspoon powdered mustard

1/8 teaspoon nutmeg

3 cups shredded sharp cheddar cheese

1/2 teaspoon salt

1/2 teaspoon pepper

1/2 cup shredded Parmesan

DIRECTIONS

• Preheat the oven to 375°F. Lightly butter a large rectangular casserole pan or 4 to 6 individual ovenproof dishes (such as ramekins).

• Cook the pasta in salted boiling water according to package directions. Drain, return to pot, and set aside.

• In a medium pot, melt the butter over medium-high heat.

• Sprinkle in the flour, stirring until a sticky dough forms. Cook, whisking constantly, for 1 to 2 minutes.

• Slowly pour in the milk, continuing to whisk, until a thick white sauce forms.

• Whisk in the powdered mustard and nutmeg.

• Gradually add the cheddar cheese, whisking as you go, until smooth.

• Add the salt and pepper and cook for an additional 1 to 2 minutes, continuing to whisk.

• Use a spatula to scrape the sauce into the cooked pasta and stir gently until all pasta is coated.

• Transfer the pasta-cheese mixture into the prepared pan or dishes and top with the shredded Parmesan.

• Bake for 20 to 25 minutes, or until the cheese on top bubbles and is lightly browned in spots.

• Serve hot.

SERVES 6

EASIEST ROAST CHICKEN TO TRICK SOMEONE INTO FALLING IN LOVE WITH YOU

GLM

Cooking for someone you're hoping to hop into bed with, or at least make out with on the couch, or do something in between with, can be daunting. Between choosing what to cook and getting it done and the kitchen cleaned up before your date arrives (or, alternately, cooking it while he or she sips wine and flirts with you while you try to keep from burning the side dish), it can be a lot to manage.

This recipe is your solution. Unless your paramour is a vegetarian, this is the absolute best thing you can make to inspire your lover to fall madly in love with you. Just about every meat-eater likes chicken, and this is chicken in its most glorious form: roasted whole, until the skin turns crispy, the meat gets juicy, and your house smells homey, in a way that will make your paramour feel hungry and excited, yet relaxed. In other words: primed for love.

Do your shopping early to avoid last-minute dinner jitters. If it's a weekday, perhaps go to the supermarket before work. Then when you get home, you'll already feel like something is done. You can have more time to shower and send your friends selfies of your perfect "I'm staying in, but I'm still very adorable" outfit.

Get the chicken prepped and into the oven before homeboy (or homegirl) arrives, roast some sweet potatoes or whip up some risotto (page 63), and throw together a simple green salad. Open the wine so it has a chance to breathe, and wipe down the counters. Then get ready for your date. Design a lighting scheme, spray your house with Febreze, etc.

Best-case scenario: Your honey takes one bite of a succulent piece of chicken, gazes into your eyes, and declares his or her undying affection. Worst-case scenario: It doesn't work out, and your date takes off, leaving you with the best chicken of your life. Either way, you're in good company.

EASIEST ROAST CHICKEN TO TRICK SOMEONE INTO FALLING IN LOVE WITH YOU

INGREDIENTS

1 whole (4- to 5-pound) roasting chicken, giblets removed

½ cup extra-virgin olive oil

12 cloves garlic, chopped

Leaves from 2 sprigs fresh rosemary

1 lemon, zested and thinly sliced

2 teaspoons salt

2 teaspoons pepper

DIRECTIONS

- Preheat the oven to 425°F.

- Rinse the chicken under cool running water and pat dry with paper towels. Place it in a large (at least 9 x 13-inch) casserole pan or a cast iron pan (this is my preferred pan for roasting a chicken).

- In a small bowl, whisk together the olive oil, garlic, rosemary, lemon zest, salt, and pepper. (You can also leave the garlic cloves whole and blend these ingredients together in a food processor or blender.)

- Pour a bit of the oil-garlic mixture into the cupped palm of your hand and rub it over the skin of the chicken.

- Gently slide your hands between the skin and the flesh of the chicken and rub some of the oil mixture beneath the skin. Pour a bit more oil into your hands and rub the cavity of the chicken with it. Continue until the whole chicken is covered with the garlic-oil mixture.

- Place a few slices of lemon between the skin and the flesh. Stuff the rest of the slices into the cavity. Arrange the chicken breast-side up in the pan.

- Cover the pan tightly with aluminum foil.

- Bake covered for 30 minutes.

- Remove the foil and bake uncovered for another 25 to 30 minutes, or until the skin is golden brown and the juices run clear (stick a knife into the thigh to check this).

- Cut into pieces and serve hot.

- Watch as your dinner guest slowly melts before your eyes.

SERVES 4

HEARTBREAK HAMBURGERS

MPB

Hi, heartbroken hotties,

I love you. I send you a hug.

There is no cure for heartbreak, except heroin, I bet.

And I don't really think heartbreak gets any easier with time. There are of course different levels of it, but it's fucking awful and painful and that's that. It always hits me very hard, whether it was a real romance or just two months (or days) of dating. I can't handle rejection. My parents loved me too hard and my ego is hanging by a tiny little shaving of a fingernail.

I also love to romanticize sadness. I'll start to cry if I see a roll of condoms in my drawer. *Oh, he'll never come back to use those . . .* (I then poke holes in them just in case he does!)

There's that beer he was drinking right before he ended it. I'll leave it there open, hoping he'll come back to finish it. Fuck the flies. Or maybe I'll finish it to be close to him. Again, fuck the flies.

There are those pajamas he'll never get to see. Maybe I should return them? No, I'm sad. I deserve them.

When I'm wallowing, what I like to do is throw on sneakers, grab my credit card, and leave my house in a rage. I pretend I'm going for a run and just stop and buy the most expensive item possible in the closest proximity to my home. I then leave the store and start to weep openly in the street. Perhaps a friend will call and I'll ignore it. I need the stare of these random strangers before I consult with my real confidants.

The dream of course is that I'll faint on a grassy knoll. (I've never fainted and all the glamorous people get to faint.) The most dramatic way to faint is definitely after a breakup. Either that or onstage during a high school play because you haven't eaten enough, but my chances for that are gone.

My purchase may or may not have been stolen during my dramatic faint, but it's okay if it was; that would only add to my damsel-in-distress vibe. In my fantasy, I now run into someone I know. I don't necessarily know them well, but we've met once or twice and we've had some sort of connection (at least in my mind). This person doesn't have to be a man, although perhaps, ideally, it is. It could also be a close friend's kindly aunt, or the salesperson I've just stolen from. A breakup is a good time to make amends in other parts of your life.

This person will pick me up, buy me some old-timey self-help book full of wizardry, and then take me out for a light drink that I've never heard of. They will take me home, hug me tightly, and tell me everything will be okay. They will check in with me the next morning. And we'll develop some kind of friendship where I help them in the future.

This is just a fantasy, though, and it's clear what it means. I don't want to deal with my real life, I want some romantic guardian angel to come in and walk me home and save me. Instead what happens is I go home, still in tears, maybe having taken a few crying selfies to send to friends to show them just how sad I am. I call my mom. I get in bed. I cry and cry and then I go to work the next day. Never in my life have I taken a personal day, no matter how much I've wanted to.

So we're giving you Heartbreak Hamburgers instead of Heartbreak Hot Fudge Sundaes or Heartbreak Kill Yourself Chocolate Cake or Heartbreak Starve Yourself Silly Diet. You probably have some go-to ice cream dessert (if not, try our Schadenfreude Sundae on page 89!), but we want to remind you that you're strong. You're gonna be okay. So instead of engaging in some terrible shopping causing buyer's remorse, like me, go out and buy the ingredients for these hamburgers. Let your friends come over, if you can, and let them help you cook.

Or just sit in front of your TV weeping, because that's important too. I often lose my appetite when I'm heartbroken, so maybe try to cook these to get your protein. Or leave them as a goal: When you feel strong enough, you'll invite some friends over for burgers and beers. You'll have a mental picture of yourself being there and somehow you will get there. If this book has one goal, it's to give you a way to make your life a little better by teaching you how to take care of yourself. This heartbroken time is when you most need to take care of yourself. You have to pull yourself out of it. You've got to be strong like a hamburger (or maybe Hamburglar in my case).

Until then, scream out in the streets like you're Cate Blanchett in *Blue Jasmine.*

You're allowed to. And it's fun. Plus, if you've never fainted glamorously, then frankly you deserve it. I still hope I get my chance. Pray for me.

HEARTBREAK HAMBURGERS

INGREDIENTS

1 pound lean ground beef

½ white onion, finely chopped

4 cloves garlic, minced, divided

1 chipotle pepper (from a can, packed in adobo sauce), finely chopped, plus 1–2 spoonfuls of the adobo sauce

6 ounces medium or sharp cheddar, cut into ½-inch cubes

½ teaspoon salt, plus more for aioli

½ teaspoon pepper, plus more for aioli

¼ cup mayonnaise

1 handful fresh cilantro leaves, very finely chopped

Fresh tomato, sliced

Lettuce, sliced

DIRECTIONS

• Preheat grill or a frying pan (preferably cast iron) to medium-high heat.

• Oil or spray lightly to avoid sticking.

• In a mixing bowl, combine the beef, the onion, 2 cloves' worth of the garlic, the chipotle pepper and adobo sauce, the cheddar, and the salt and pepper. Mix well, using your hands.

• Shape the mixture into 4 patties.

• Grill the patties for 3 to 4 minutes on each side (at least long enough to melt the cheese).

• While the burgers cook, whisk together the remaining 2 cloves' worth of garlic, the mayonnaise, the cilantro, and more salt and pepper to taste. Set aside.

• Serve the burgers on buns or on their own, with tomato and lettuce, topped with a dollop of the aioli.

SERVES 4

NETFLIX AND CHILI CON CARNE

GLM

As far as I am concerned, the best part of falling in love is not the first can't-get-'em-out-of-your-head, smiling-all-the-time dopey lust part. It's not even first-, second-, or third-time sex. No. The best part is the settling in, the getting comfortable. That magical time when you discover intimacy in the little moments of your days and nights together. You start wearing your sweatpants around each other (okay, your cutest sweatpants, but still) and really getting into the pleasures of lounging around together. Perhaps one of the most noteworthy hallmarks of this special time is when you find a show to watch together. It becomes your thing. Maybe just one or two episodes together on weeknights, but the occasional cozy Sunday afternoon can be spent snuggled on the couch, computer on a pillow between you, clicking "Next Episode" after "Next Episode" until your eyes hurt from the weird computer light. But it's okay, because your collective eyes hurt together. You make the commitment to never watch the next episode without the other person (the ultimate betrayal). Things get serious.

It's tempting to make your binge-watching evenings and afternoons (or mornings—we won't judge) also takeout binge-eating events, but we think a big pot of flavorful, spicy chili is a much better bet. First of all, it requires very little attention. Second, it contains plenty of protein to give you long-lasting stamina for your show-streaming fest. Finally, home cooking is very conducive to the kind of snuggly settling in that Netflix-bingeing tends to encourage. Why not use it to your advantage?

Oh, and the toppings are purely optional, but we think they put the chili over the top. You should definitely consider serving at least one or two of them.

Oh, and have sex before you eat the chili. Duh.

NETFLIX AND CHILI CON CARNE

INGREDIENTS

1 pound lean ground beef

1 large onion, chopped

2 cloves garlic, crushed

1 tablespoon chili powder

1 teaspoon ground cumin

1 teaspoon dried oregano leaves

1 teaspoon unsweetened cocoa powder

½ teaspoon salt

½ teaspoon hot sauce

1 (28-ounce) can diced tomatoes, with their juice

1 (16-ounce) can red kidney beans, drained and rinsed

Optional toppings: shredded cheddar cheese, sour cream, chopped green or white onions, chopped cilantro

DIRECTIONS

- In a 3-quart saucepan, cook the beef, onion, and garlic over medium-high heat, stirring occasionally, until beef is brown, about 8 minutes.

- Stir in the remaining ingredients except for the beans and bring the mixture to a boil. Reduce heat to low, cover, and simmer for 1 hour, stirring occasionally.

- Stir in the beans and bring the chili back to a boil. Reduce the heat to low again and simmer uncovered, stirring occasionally, for about 20 minutes, or until the chili reaches your desired thickness.

- Serve hot in bowls, with any of the optional toppings.

SERVES 4

I LOVE YOU TIRAMISU

GLM & MPB

Some of us are ready to say I love you after one whirlwind weekend of romance. If this is you, we are impressed. You are cool and bohemian like Jessa on *Girls*. Some of us have a very hard time saying it. If this is you, you are cool too, like the Miranda writing this book. (And yes, the Miranda from *Sex and the City*.) No matter what your disposition, dessert is a great way to say "I'm in love with you."

That said, a big part of growing up is learning how to speak your mind. Hopefully you can serve this dessert and say how you feel, but if you're not there yet, tiramisu will speak the words you can't.

The brilliant thing about tiramisu is that it's really a dish that gets assembled, rather than baked. Try your best, but do not fear if your masterpiece does not look perfect. That is in and of itself kind of adorable. Even lovelier, this recipe is for making individual tiramisus, so you don't have to fuss with spatulas or plates (you're telling your boo that you love them—you already have enough to worry about).

I LOVE YOU TIRAMISU

INGREDIENTS

1 cup heavy cream, divided (no, you may not use Cool Whip)

4 tablespoons sugar, divided

4 ounces mascarpone (Italian cream cheese) or cream cheese, at room temperature

½ teaspoon vanilla extract

6 ladyfingers (Because this is a LADYLIKE dessert! But vanilla wafer cookies, like Nilla Wafers, will work in a pinch.)

½ cup strong black coffee

½ teaspoon unsweetened cocoa powder

DIRECTIONS

- Have two 8-ounce wineglasses ready. These are not for drinking, so put aside two more for that. (You're working up the nerve to say "I love you.")

- In a chilled bowl, combine ½ cup of the heavy cream and 2 tablespoons of the sugar. Whip with a hand mixer, electric beater, or whisk until soft peaks form (7 to 8 minutes, with an electric implement, 10 to 12 minutes if using a whisk). Cover and refrigerate until ready to use.

- In a large bowl, combine ½ cup of the heavy cream, the remaining 2 tablespoons of sugar, the mascarpone or cream cheese, and the vanilla extract. Whip with a hand mixer until light and fluffy. Set aside.

- Reserve 2 ladyfingers for garnish, and snap or cut the remaining ladyfingers in half.

- Taking 2 halves at time, dip them quickly into the coffee and drop them into the bottom of a wineglass. Repeat with the other wineglass.

- Put a heaping tablespoon of the mascarpone/cream cheese mixture on top of the ladyfingers in each glass.

- Add another layer of ladyfingers dipped in coffee, another of the cream cheese mixture, then 1 more layer of ladyfingers.

- Top with remaining mascarpone/cream cheese mixture and dollop with the whipped cream.

- Break the reserved 2 ladyfingers in half and insert 2 halves into the top of each glass.

- Put the cocoa powder in a sieve or strainer and tap it gently over each glass to dust the top.

- Refrigerate for at least 1 hour before serving.

- Be in love. Love is dope. Love.

SERVES 2

EAT YOUR ENEMY CRISPY TREATS

GLM & MPB

And for our last recipe . . . we're giving you cannibalism!

No, we're not, obviously, but we are closing the book out with one of our favorite things: revenge. When there are no more tears to cry, the object of your fury is no longer answering your text messages, and you're just mad as hell, take your anger out on a crispy rice treat version of him or her.

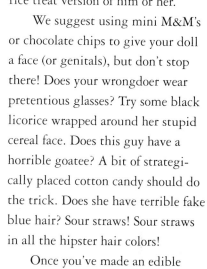

We suggest using mini M&M's or chocolate chips to give your doll a face (or genitals), but don't stop there! Does your wrongdoer wear pretentious glasses? Try some black licorice wrapped around her stupid cereal face. Does this guy have a horrible goatee? A bit of strategically placed cotton candy should do the trick. Does she have terrible fake blue hair? Sour straws! Sour straws in all the hipster hair colors!

Once you've made an edible version or your ex or enemy, it's time to get all Norman Bates on it. We stabbed our marshmallow monster with toothpicks and a steak knife, but if you have other sharp objects, you should use them; be a creative stabber. Thumbtacks, a letter opener, old earrings, a (clean) cuticle cutter, or a lancet will all do the trick! You can also beat up your treat with a rolling pin or a hammer—it'll still be tasty afterward.

Then enjoy eating your enemy—bite by bite. Say good-bye to your relationship in a very meaningful spiritual way. This human is dead to you (or at least its doll version is).

EAT YOUR ENEMY CRISPY TREATS

INGREDIENTS

3 tablespoons unsalted butter, plus more to coat the pan (or use cooking spray)

1 (10-ounce) package marshmallows (or use 4 cups miniature marshmallows)

6 cups crispy rice cereal

Miniature candy-coated chocolate pieces or chocolate chips, for decorating

DIRECTIONS

• Grease a 13 × 9 × 2-inch baking pan with butter or line with parchment or wax paper.

• In a large saucepan, melt the butter over low heat. Add the marshmallows and stir until completely melted, 5 to 7 minutes. Remove from heat.

• Add the crispy rice cereal to the saucepan. Stir until the marshmallows and cereal are combined.

• Using a buttered spatula, parchment or wax paper, or your buttered hands, evenly press the mixture into the prepared pan. Let cool for 15 minutes.

• Use a sharp knife to trace the outline of a person (don't worry if it's not perfect—the person you're replicating here obviously isn't perfect either).

• Create a face with the candy-coated chocolate pieces or chocolate chips, as desired.

• Poke all over with toothpicks or other sharp tools until you feel better.

SERVES 8 TO 10

CONCLUSION

Congratulations on completing your *Hot Mess Kitchen* education! We assume you are now seasoned chefs and likely opening up your own restaurants, or food trucks, or food smart cars, or whatever the hell is cool at this exact moment in time. We bet you're also healed of all your emotional problems and cured of any bad behavior or millennial woes. Great, us too! Everyone gets an A-plus. Tell your self-esteem we said so.

Truly, we hope you have had / are having at least half as much fun reading our stories and cooking our recipes as we have had writing and preparing them. This cookbook has made each of us feel like a little bit less of a hot mess in the practical sense (we had deadlines and responsibility), and Miranda actually became a dignified cook. But in a more meaningful way, we had to look at our lives and examine them so we could share them with you. We had to figure out what recipes we actually used and thought would be helpful to other people. We had to take stock of our lives, and that has made us feel better. We also think you will relate to everything in this book, so that makes us feel closer to you and less alone. Being a hot mess is really hard sometimes, so it's nice to be reminded that everyone kind of is one.

We hope you take this book with you from apartment to house to home to wherever you go and that these recipes become staples in your life moving forward. Sometimes you'll be a hot mess; sometimes you'll be really clean. During all of these times our recipes will be with you. Remember, Abandonment Issues Apple Pie can also just be the apple pie you cook for your hypothetical children down the line. (Try not to give those children abandonment issues.)

And now, dear friends, we must bid you adieu because of page count reasons, and also because we've taught you everything we know. Literally, we don't know anything else and would have nothing else to say.

We love you and we hope you love us too because we still need validation, and we're not above that kind of thing.

XOXO,

Gabi and Miranda

P.S. You do love us, right?

P.P.S. Whatever, we don't care. We're chill. Don't love us. NBD.

P.P.P.S. No, but actually can you let us know somehow that you love us? We do need to know.

P.P.P.P.S. FORGET IT, WE LOVE YOU REGARDLESS AND NOW ARE GOING TO BAKE A FRIENDSHIP CAKE TOGETHER. BYE!

ACKNOWLEDGMENTS

Thank you to B. J. Novak and Dev Flaherty for creating Li.st, so we could meet on it, become friends, and realize we should write a book together. To Sophia Rossi for believing in us and introducing us to our amazing book agent, Richard Abate. To Richard, for guiding and advocating for us every step of the way. To Rachel Kim, whose intuition, persistence, and organization made this entire process better and smoother. To our extraordinary editor, Maddie Caldwell, who couldn't have been a more perfect fit for this. She just "gets it," and also picks fantastic places to meet for drinks in New York. We feel cool knowing her. To Elizabeth Van Itallie for making our brainchild look and feel better than we ever dreamed it could. To everyone at Grand Central / Hachette, including Becky Maines, Morgan Hedden, Kallie Shimek, and Tom Whatley, for making *Hot Mess Kitchen* available to the masses. We love you.

To Mindy Kaling for adding her name to this project and providing us with so much support (on a daily basis for Miranda) and also for just adding general coolness points to this cookbook (it's cool, we know seeing her name on the cover helped you decide to buy this—we're okay with that).

To Frankie Frankeny, whose beautiful photography brought our book to life, and whose dry humor and very cute dog (you're in our hearts forever, Pie) made our photo shoot the best. We also thank her for dealing with our vanity and insistence that we look as hot as possible in every photo. On that subject, thanks to Kristina Welzien (styleseat.com/kristina) for making our hair and makeup gorgeous, and to Dena Smith (leowithcancer.com) for bringing her entire closet to style us for our photos, and teaching us how to pose. We also want to mention Nada Perrone, Steve Smith, Rebecca Kee, Brian Cristol, Irvin Lin, Chris Jackson, and Haylee Bay for lending their beautiful faces to the shoot. Without them, it would look like we have no friends. Thank you also to Kellye Gray for opening her home to us for several of our photos.

FROM MIRANDA

Thank you to my parents, Russell and Anita Berman, for birthing me, believing in me, and also for picking up my late-night panicked phone calls even though I should probably be calling other people at this stage in my life. Thank you, as well, to my sister for generally being there and for having cute children, of whom it is fun to look at photos and smile.

Hillary Reinsberg, thank you for being a lifelong pal and also for lending your editing smarts to a bunch of early drafts of my essays. Everyone at *The Mindy Project*, especially all the assistants, deserves a special mention for listening to me talk and complain about how itchy I am. I love you all.

Finally and most importantly, I want to thank Gabi, for trusting me enough to work with, for texting me back when no one else would, for being a friend, and of course, for teaching me how the hell to cook. I love you.

FROM GABI

Thank you to my wonderful family, Ouisue Packard, Larry Moskowitz, Jeremy Moskowitz, Jennifer Truax, Alan, Kathy and Haran Wolkenstein. Your support means the world to me.

To Barry Kotler and Lisa Shotland, thank you for your belief in me. I feel so lucky to have agents who are also awesome friends.

To my smart, sexy, dapper husband, Evan, thank you for letting me ramble about this book for a year and a half, even though we had a wedding to plan. Thank you for letting me test recipes on you and leave you with the dishes. Thank you for cheering me on at every turn. I love you more than anything.

And to my sweet, beautiful, brilliant coauthor Miranda, thank you for patiently listening to my rants, for making me laugh, for making our book hilarious, and for teaching me how to use Snapchat. I love you forever.

INDEX

Page numbers of photographs appear in italics.

ABOUT THE AUTHORS

Gabi Moskowitz is the editor in chief of the nationally acclaimed budget cooking blog *BrokeAss Gourmet* and the author of four cookbooks.

Gabi is also the coproducer of *Young & Hungry*, a Freeform comedy currently in its fifth season, inspired by her life and writing. She starred in a web series in conjunction with the show, called *Young & Foodie*.

When she is not blogging, writing books, or making television, Gabi contributes to the *Washington Post*, the *Guardian*, and *Lenny Letter*. She lives in San Francisco with her husband, Evan.

Miranda Berman is a TV writer who has spent the majority of her career working on *The Mindy Project*. She also hosts a podcast aptly titled *High School with Miranda Berman*, on which she interviews guests about their high school experiences. She's originally from New York City, but currently lives and eats in Los Angeles.